# THE WORLD ALMANAC®
# ALMANAC®
## GUIDE TO
# GETTING
# OUT ALIVE

# THE WORLD ALMANAC®

# GUIDE TO
# GETTING
# OUT ALIVE

## 1,001 TIPS FOR SURVIVING
### EXTREME WEATHER, KILLER BEES, DENTIST VISITS, ANNOYING SIBLINGS, AND OTHER MAJOR THREATS

WORLD ALMANAC BOOKS

World Almanac books may be purchased in bulk at special discounts for sales promotion, corporate gifts, fund-raising, or educational purposes. Special editions can also be created to specifications. For details, contact the Special Sales Department, 307 West 36th Street, 11th Floor, New York, NY 10018 or info@skyhorsepublishing.com.

Published by World Almanac Books, an imprint of Skyhorse Publishing, Inc., 307 West 36th Street, 11th Floor, New York, NY 10018.

The World Almanac® is a registered trademark of Skyhorse Publishing, Inc. All rights reserved.

www.skyhorsepublishing.com
Please follow our publisher Tony Lyons on Instagram @tonylyonsisuncertain

10 9 8 7 6 5 4 3 2 1

Text by Joanne Mattern
Cover design by Kai Texel

Library of Congress Cataloging-in-Publication Data is available on file.

Print ISBN: 978-1-5107-7792-7
Ebook ISBN: 978-1-5107-7793-4

Printed in China

# CONTENTS

# INTRODUCTION

The world is a wild, exhilarating place. One minute, life is going along great, or at least it's not terrible. The next, you're fighting off a rampaging shark, watching a tornado heading straight toward you, or suffering from serious FGD (Friend Group Drama). What's a person to do?

Here's a secret: The answer to dealing with most problems comes down to two simple words: Be Prepared! Life can throw lots of roadblocks and challenges in your way. But if you're prepared and have a plan to solve your problem, you have a much better chance of getting out in one piece, with a brighter day ahead of you. And that's exactly what this book is about.

Problems come in many forms. You might be fighting with your parents or teachers, or dealing with bullies. You might go on a hike that goes wrong and leaves you stranded miles from home. You might have bad skin or body odor. You might be faced with a natural disaster or a terrible accident. Whatever it is, we've got you covered!

In the pages of this book, you'll find hundreds of tips and tricks that could save your life, or at least save your sanity. We've gathered first aid and survival basics, as well as advice and explanations for common—and not so common—disasters. So whether you're nervous about trying out for the school play, facing a serious personal crisis, or in physical danger, chances are this book will help you out.

Life is a wild ride. Are you ready to hop onboard? Open the pages of this book and find out how to get out alive!

# SURVIVAL SKILLS IOI

# In Trouble? STOP!

Stranded? Lost? Don't panic! Instead, **STOP: S**top, **T**hink, **O**bserve, **P**lan.

### 1. Stop.
As soon as you realize you're lost, stop everything. Don't panic, run around screaming, or fling yourself into the bushes to try to break a new trail. Instead, take a deep breath or two (or twelve!), and try to relax. You need a clear head to make sensible decisions that will get you home as soon as possible.

### 2. Think.
Your mind is your best survival tool. Think about where you are. Use your map or compass to figure out your location. A map should show streams, mountains, and other natural landmarks that can help you orient yourself. Visualize any memorable features you saw on the way to the spot where you are now: landmarks, trail markers, that weird flowering tree. Most of all, stay where you are, and stay with others in your group.

### 3. Observe.
Look around. Are your surroundings safe? If you're on the edge of a cliff, or a storm is coming, or you see a big bear headed your way, the answer is no! Find a safe shelter right away. Once you're safe, continue to observe. Where is a good spot to build a sturdier shelter? Is there an open area or a big hill where you could signal for help? Observe yourself too. Are you okay, or do you need first aid? If there are other people with you, observe their condition as well and apply any necessary first aid.

## 4. Plan.

Your priorities should be:

- Shelter
- Fire
- Signaling
- Water

Gather materials to build a shelter and get to work making your new home. Figure out how to signal for help. Check out your food and water supplies. If you are in a group, assign jobs to each person. Remember that most lost people are found within 24 hours. You'll be home, sleeping in your own bed, in no time!

> ⚠ **SAFETY TIP: Lost and Found?**
>
> It's tempting to keep moving to find your way back home sooner. But a lot of the time, the best thing to do is stay in one place as soon as you realize you're lost. If you don't know why you got lost in the first place or have a visible landmark to head toward, it's way too easy to follow the wrong trail and end up even more lost. And staying in one place means that a search party is more likely to find you (or your signals) while performing a thorough grid search.

# Here I Am!
# (Signaling for Help)

When you're lost and want to be found, you need to let searchers know where you are! Here are some ways to bring attention to yourself.

- If you have a cellphone and can get service, call 911. Describe where you are, using any landmarks you can recall, even if you haven't seen them for awhile.
- If your phone's battery is low, sending a text message uses less energy than a call.
- Carry a locator beacon. These work even without cell service.
- Use a mirror to reflect sunlight—even the glassy surface of a phone or a tablet can sometimes work in a pinch. Searchers will hopefully see the flash. Rescuers flying overhead may be able to see the light. You can buy special mirrors for signaling from a camping or sporting goods store. Metal, such as a belt buckle, canteen, or tool kit, can also be used to reflect light send a sun signal.
- Send an SOS with a flashlight. Block the light with your hand, on and off, to signal three short, three long, and three short bursts of light.
- Make noise! Use a whistle to alert rescuers. Three short blasts is the universal distress signal. As a bonus, the extra noise may make animals steer clear!

- Find a clear area and use rocks or logs to make a large X or V shape that might be spotted by aerial searchers. Or spell out "Help" or "SOS."
- Build a signal fire in a clear area. Be aware that a big signal fire will need a LOT of wood and careful monitoring.

⚠ **SAFETY TIP: Dress for Success**

What you wear can have a big effect on staying comfortable and alive. Layers are a good way to regulate body temperature. Synthetic materials are good at retaining body heat, and so are wool and flannel. Be sure to have a waterproof jacket or poncho to protect yourself from wind, water, and cold. And your shoes and socks shouldn't be an afterthought. Make sure you pick them out with the season, climate, terrain, and planned activities in mind.

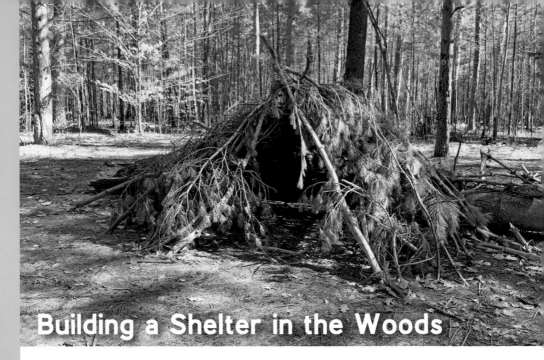

# Building a Shelter in the Woods

It's important to protect yourself from the elements—heat, cold, precipitation, even sun. Building a shelter should be your first priority when you're stranded outdoors. Here's how to build a shelter in the woods:

### I. Find the Right Spot.
Make like you're Goldilocks, and look for a place that's "just right." The most important thing is that the area is dry. No one wants to sit or sleep on soggy ground! Higher ground is usually better than low spots. Trees can shelter you from a cold wind.

### 2. Make Your Bed.
You don't want to sleep directly on the cold ground. Gather leaves, pine needles, and bark, and make a big pile. Your new bed should be as long as you are tall and several feet deep. Snuggle into your new bed—it will help you conserve body heat and stay warm.

### 3. Look for Natural Shelter.
A fallen tree that has enough room for you to crawl under makes a great start to a shelter. A big rock or overhang can also provide a good place to call home.

### 4. Build It Up.

You'll want to make your shelter as secure and protective as possible. Look for fallen branches, or cut down some yourself, and lean them against the fallen tree or rock to make a wall. You want your shelter to be small so it will retain your body heat.

### 5. Heat It Up.

If cold temperatures are a concern, don't worry about everyone in your group having their own beds and privacy—just make sure the shelter is big enough for all. Staying together is the best way to stay warm.

### 6. Make a Lean-To.

If there are no fallen trees to use as a base, you can make a lean-to. Place a long stick against a tree or rock and prop it up by tying smaller branches together in an upside-down V shape. Lean more sticks against the rest of the long branch, then pile leaves and branches on top of them to finish your shelter.

### 7. Tents and Trees.

If you brought a tent, bravo! You can set it up for shelter. If you didn't, a rope and a space blanket, poncho, or tarp can be made into a tent. Find two trees that are close together and tie the rope between them. Then drape the tarp over the middle of the rope and weigh down the edges with rocks. Voila—you've made a tent!

# Building a Shelter in the Snow

### DIY Snow Shelter

- Pile up snow until it's six to eight feet high.
- Shape the pile into a dome or mound to prevent it from collapsing.
- Poke several long branches through the middle of your pile to use as guides.
- Poke sticks, about as long as a 12-inch ruler, all around the outside of your shelter, placing them one to two feet apart.
- Wait at least 15 minutes for the snow to harden. (It will have melted a bit from your moving and touching it.)
- Dig an entrance to your shelter on the downhill side.
- Continue digging into the center of the snow pile. Remove snow until you reach the guide sticks you placed earlier.
- Congratulations—you've reached the center!
- Make a hole in the top of your shelter to allow fresh air to flow through.
- Make sure you mark the entrance in case it gets covered in snow.
- Keep a small shovel inside the shelter, just in case. You may need to dig your way out of a collapse.

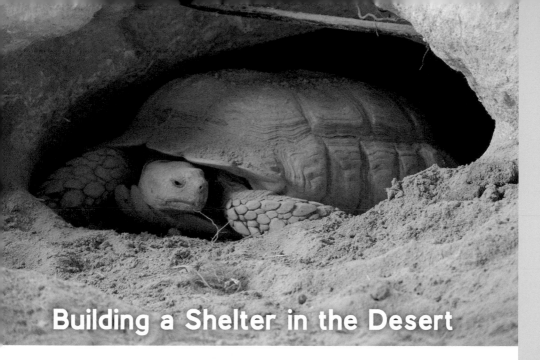

# Building a Shelter in the Desert

### DIY Desert Shelter

- Find four long branches. Branches that are three to five feet long are best.
- Drive the branches into the ground about five feet apart to make a square.
- Tie rope or cord between the branches. If you don't have rope, try using vines or long grass. You don't want anything too heavy.
- Drape a tarp across the top of the branches to make a roof. Weigh the corners down with flat, thin rocks.
- If branches aren't an option, use terrain features such as rock clusters, sand mounds, or depressions between dunes as the structure for your covering.

> ⚠ **SAFETY TIP: Terrible Places to Build a Shelter**
>
> - The edge of a cliff
> - A swamp
> - Next to running water
> - A dry riverbed or ravine
> - Next to a bear den or venomous snake nest

# How to Build a Fire

A fire is a must if you want to stay warm. Here's how to build a roaring blaze.

### 1. Safety First!
The first rule of fire-building is to find a safe place to build. If you set the woods on fire, you'll have a much bigger problem! Look for a place that is away from trees, bushes, and grass. A patch of bare dirt, sand, or gravel is best. If there is no spot of bare ground, make one by digging up the grass. Then place the dirt in a pile in the center of your fire patch. A pile of dirt about four inches deep will do. If you can, lay rocks around your fire patch to make it extra safe.

### 2. Gather Tinder.
Tinder is extra-dry material that catches fire fast. Think of leaves, grass, pine needles, and small pieces of bark. Again, make sure your tinder is dry—wet tinder just doesn't work. Experienced campers even bring dryer lint, newspaper, brown paper bags, or commercial tinder from home. Pile your tinder in the middle of your fire patch.

### 3. Kindle the Flame.
Big logs don't catch fire easily and can smother a little flame, so you have to start small. After the tinder, make sure you have twigs and sticks to use as kindling.

### 4. Fuel the Fire.
Next you need some bigger branches to keep your fire burning. Again, big fat logs are not the best choice. Go for branches that you can easily cut using your pocketknife.

## 5. Build a Teepee.

No, not the kind of teepee you sleep in. We're talking about a teepee of wood. Stack your kindling above your tinder in a teepee, or pyramid, shape, leaving space between the branches for air to circulate. Then stack your bigger fuel branches in a tent shape above the kindling.

## 6. Light It Up!

Don't rely on rubbing two sticks together to start a fire. That works great in old cartoons, but in real life, not so much. Instead, use a match, a lighter, or flint and tinder. Set the flame to your tinder and let it burn. As the fire consumes the kindling, add more fuel branches to keep the fire going.

> ⚠ **SAFETY TIP: Fire Extinguisher**
> Knowing how to safely put out a fire is as important as finding the safest place to build it to begin with. Sprinkle water over the fire, stirring the embers and ashes gently with a stick as you do. Stirring will expose hot spots to the water so everything can be extinguished. Wait until steam stops rising. Then place the back of your hand near the ashes (not IN the ashes!) to check for heat. If the ashes are still hot, pour more water over them until the fire is truly out.

# But I'm Starving! (What to Eat in the Wild)

So you've finished your stash of granola bars and jerky, and you're feeling really hungry. While most plants are perfectly safe to eat, some could make you really sick—or worse! So before you reach for those yummy-looking berries or mushrooms, stop and look for clues that tell you if a plant is safe to eat.

- Consider taking a class in foraging for wild plants.
- Bring a plant identification guidebook on your hike. You'll have the information and pictures you need right at your fingertips.
- Use your sense of smell. Wild onion is a common plant that is safe and tasty. Take a sniff and you'll know if the plant you see is an onion.
- On the other hand, an almond smell is a sign that the plant can contain cyanide, which you definitely don't want to snack on.
- Avoid mushrooms. Unless you're well informed, many are risky—and they can look very similar to the delicious kind!
- Stay away from plants that have a milky sap, waxy leaves, fine hairs or spines, white berries, or umbrella-shaped flowers. These are all common traits of toxic plants.
- Tree nuts and berries will fill you up faster and taste better than grass or leaves.
- Test an unfamiliar plant by rubbing it on the skin of your inner elbow. Wait a few minutes to see if there is a skin reaction.
- Take a small bite. If the plant tastes soapy or bitter, or it makes your tongue numb or itchy, spit it out and rinse your mouth with water.
- Aquatic plants, such as cattails, are generally safe to eat.
- Remember that not all parts of a plant may be edible. The flowers may taste good, while the leaves or roots might be poisonous. So handle—and eat—with care.

# On the Right Track

Animal tracks can be useful to know when you're out in the wild. You might follow tracks to find food. For example, deer love vegetation, so deer tracks could lead to you a tasty treat. Animal tracks can also alert you to danger. If you spot bear or cougar tracks, you should probably head the other way!

Where can you find tracks? Look for wet, muddy areas, or areas covered with snow. You can also track animals by looking for broken vegetation or grass that has been pushed down where an animal lay down for a nap.

Here's something gross: You can also track animals by their poop! Don't think of it as stinky waste, think of poop as a clue as to what animals are nearby, and what they've been eating.

Here are some common animal tracks in North America. Note that these illustrations are not done to scale with one another—that would be a pretty big squirrel!

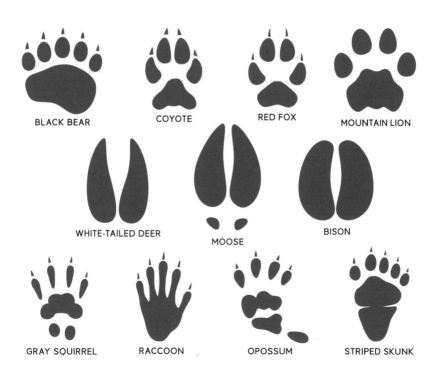

BLACK BEAR  COYOTE  RED FOX  MOUNTAIN LION

WHITE-TAILED DEER  MOOSE  BISON

GRAY SQUIRREL  RACCOON  OPOSSUM  STRIPED SKUNK

# Finding Drinkable Water

Water is much more important than food when you're stranded. A person can survive three weeks without food, but only three days without water. Here's how to find hydration in the wilderness.

- Resist the urge to drink from streams, lakes, or rivers. The water may look clear and clean, but it may have nasty bacteria that can make you very sick. You don't know what nearby runoff—a chemical factory or a cattle feedlot—might be feeding that stream.
- Pack water purifying tablets or a purifying kit. Using these products is the only way to make water safe to drink.
- If you have a camping stove or fire, you can boil water to purify it.
- Rainwater is not perfectly clean, but it's usually a better choice than water from a puddle or pond. Any container can be used to collect rain as it's falling. Or lay a tarp or plastic sheet across some sticks and place a rock in the center to make a rain collector.
- Suck dew from leaves and grass. (We know it sounds gross, but it could save your life!)
- Look for other sources of moisture, such as wild fruits or berries.
- Forget about drinking water from inside a cactus. That liquid is nasty and could make you sick.

## Build a Solar Still

You can gather water by building a solar still, which uses the sun to evaporate moisture out of the ground. Awesome, right? You won't get a lot of water this way, but it's better than nothing. Here's how to build one:

- Dig a hole about two feet wide and two feet deep.
- Place a container, such as a jar or bowl, in the hole.
- Cover the hole with a plastic sheet or tarp.
- Place rocks in the middle to create an inverted cone over your container.
- Wait 24 hours.
- Uncover your container, which should now hold water that evaporated from the ground and is safe to drink.

⚠ **SAFETY TIP: Is Snow Safe to Drink?**
You've probably always heard "Don't eat yellow snow!" Good advice! But if you're stranded in a snowy place, clean (not yellow, brown, or muddy) snow can be safe to drink. However, it's important to let the snow melt before consuming it.

# All Tied Up (Knot Tying 101)

What does knot tying have to do with wilderness survival? Plenty! A good knot can help you secure shelter, keep gear safe, even save someone's life! Here are three important knots to learn.

### Clove Hitch

This is the knot you'll use to tie sticks together to make a shelter.

- Bring the rope over and under the stick.
- Bring the rope around a second time. Cross it over the first wrap to make an X.
- Bring the rope end around one more time and tuck it under the center of the X.
- Pull the rope to tighten it around the stick.

⚠ **SAFETY TIP: Know Your Knots**

There are lots of knots—too many to describe here! Believe it or (k)not, entire books have been written about knot tying, and there are videos online about knots as well. So grab some rope and do your research before heading outside.

## Square Knot

This knot is good for tying gear together or for tying short ropes into a longer one.

- Lay two pieces of rope next to each other.
- Tie an overhand knot (think of this as step one from when you tie your shoes) by putting the right rope end under and over the left rope end.
- Tie another overhand knot by putting the left rope end under and over the right rope end.
- Pull the ropes tight to form the knot.

## Bowline Knot

This super-secure knot can be used to tie down tarps or pull someone to safety.

- Make a small loop in the rope.
- Bring the end of the rope through the loop, around the main part of the rope, and back down to the loop.
- Pull the main part of the rope away from the loop to tighten.

# Finding Food

Getting hungry? If the nearest McDonald's is miles away, here's how to help yourself to some fresh eats.

## Go Fish!

Streams, rivers, and ponds are full of fish. Here are some ways to catch fish in the wild.

1. Use your hands! You might be able to grab fish, frogs, or other aquatic animals out of a lake, pond, river, or stream.
2. Grab a spear. You can snag a fish using a spear or sharpened stick.
3. Use fishing line. Tie one end of the line to a metal hook (you can make one out of a bent paper clip or other piece of metal). Tie the other end to a stick to use as a pole, or tie it to a low-hanging branch if you don't want to sit around waiting for the fish to bite.
4. Look for bait. Dig up worms or grubs. If you can catch a small fish, such as a minnow, use it to bait your hook, then let it wriggle in the water to attract bigger fish.
5. If you have a net in your camping gear, wade into the water and try to scoop up or trap a fish that way.
6. Use trash to make a trap. Cut the top off a plastic bottle and place the bottle in the water facing the current. Fish can swim into the bottle, but they won't be able to swim out.
7. Look for a good spot. Many fish swim near water plants or in shallower areas of a lake or pond.

## Setting Traps
Want to trap an animal on land? Try these trapping techniques!

1. Make a simple snare by tying one end of a string or wire around a bush or low-hanging branch. Tie a loop in the other end. Place the loop in front of an animal den or along a trail. Stay out of sight (and smell) and wait for an animal to walk into the trap.

2. Make a deadfall trap. Prop a heavy rock up on sticks. (Be careful not to drop the rock on your fingers!) Place food under the rock. When the animal disturbs the sticks, the rock will fall and crush the animal. Squirrel pancake for dinner, anyone?

3. Dig a hole about 12 to 18 inches (30-45 cm) deep. Make sure the bottom is wider than the top, so the animal can't climb out. Place food scraps in the bottom of the hole for bait. You might want to prop a thin strip of bark up with twigs over the top of the hole to provide cover where an animal might try to hide—and then fall in!

> ⚠ **SAFETY TIP: Cook Before You Eat!**
> Be sure to cook anything you catch over a fire or camp stove. Raw meat or fish can contain bacteria and diseases that could make you very sick, just when you're least likely to be able to see a doctor. This is not the time to feast on sushi or steak tartare!

# Making Weapons

Are you ready to be a mighty hunter? Or perhaps you just want to defend yourself from wild animals. Either way, a weapon can be handy to have.

## Making a Spear

- Find a branch that is about as tall as you and about one inch in diameter. The branch should be hard and straight.
- Trim off any smaller branches or twigs.
- Use a pocketknife to sharpen one end of the stick into a point. Always cut away from yourself for safety.
- If you don't have a knife, sharpen the spear against a rock or other rough surface.
- If you've built a fire, hold the sharpened tip of your spear just above the flames until it changes color. This dries the wood and makes it stronger.

> ⚠ **SAFETY TIP: Don't Leave Home Without It**
> A pocketknife might not be a weapon, but it can be pretty handy in the wilderness! It's a good idea to carry a pocketknife, multitool, or Swiss army knife whenever you venture into the wild. You never know when you might need it!

## Making a Slingshot

- Find a Y-shaped branch about 6-8 inches long and 1-2 inches thick.
- Place the wood over a fire or camp stove to dry it out and make it stronger.
- Use your knife or a sharp rock to cut a shallow groove around each arm of your branch. Make each cut about an inch (2.5 cm) from the top of the sticks.
- Cut rubber bands or another stretchy material (did you bring a hair binder or scrunchie?) into two strips, each about 6-8 inches long.
- Wrap each length of rubber around a notch, then tie it on tightly with thin string or fishing line.
- Take a small piece of cloth and cut a hole near each end. Thread each length of rubber through the holes to make a pouch to hold your projectile.
- Find some rocks to use as projectiles.
- Fire away!

# Finding Your Way Using a Map and Compass

The best thing to do if you get lost is to stay where you are. But if you need to find your way out of trouble and there's no service to power your GPS, here are some tips to help you navigate like a pro!

### Navigation Tool Kit

A map and compass are your best bets to finding your way out of the wilderness.

**A topographical map**—one that shows elevations and physical features—is best. Walking across an empty field is a lot easier than getting to the other side of a forested mountain! These maps also show hills, canyons, bodies of water, and the height above sea level, all of which are useful for figuring out exactly where you are.

**A compass** is another valuable tool. The most important thing about a compass is that it can help you walk a straight line in the direction you're trying to go in. This might sound simple, but it can keep you from getting more lost as you stumble around the landscape.

## Learning to Use a Compass

- Make sure you aren't near any metal structures or objects. Metal can affect the magnetism of your compass. Watch or phone batteries can also cause interference.
- Hold out one arm and lay the compass flat on your palm. The needle will swing around to point north.
- Turn the compass dial so the orienteering arrow also points north.
- Now you should be able to find which direction is which just by looking at the compass.
- Once you've figured out what direction you want to head, follow the direction of the arrow. You can use landmarks along the trail as guides. Hike from one landmark to another, keeping an eye on the compass as you go to make sure you're headed in the right direction.

⚠ **SAFETY TIP: Practice Makes Perfect**

It's a good idea to practice using a topographical map and compass BEFORE you head out into the wild. Try it out with a friend at a local park first—or just use a map and compass to navigate your way home from a few streets over.

# Finding Your Way Using the Sun and Stars

## Sun, Moon, and Stars

**Sun.** We all know the sun rises in the east and sets in the west, right? Actually, this is not quite true. The position of the sun is affected by where you live and what season it is. However, you can use that knowledge of the sun's position as a rough guide to find east and west, and then north and south. (Here's a mnemonic, or memory trick, for remembering the compass directions: Going clockwise, "**N**ever **E**at **S**quiggly **W**orms": north, east, south, west.)

**Stars.** The stars can guide you at night. You can find the North Star by looking for the Big Dipper. That's the constellation that looks like a big ladle. If you draw an imaginary line up from the stars at the far end of the cup, you'll hit the North Star. The North Star is also the end of the "handle" of another constellation, called the Little Dipper. Why is this important? Because the North Star is the closest star to true north.

**Moon.** The moon can also be a handy guide. Here's a trick: If you draw a line from the top tip of a crescent moon to the bottom tip, that line will point roughly to the south. If the moon is big and bright, try this general rule: Between sunset and midnight, the bright side of the moon points west. Between midnight and sunrise, the bright side points east. So if you follow the direction the moon's face is pointing toward the horizon, you can locate east or west, depending on the time of night. No sun necessary! Pretty awesome, right?

## What Direction Is It?

Of course, an analog watch (the kind with an hour and minute hand on a face of numbers) tells time. But did you know it can also tell direction? Here's how to use a watch as a makeshift compass. (Note: This only works during the day in the Northern Hemisphere.)

- Hold the watch horizontally across the palm of your hand. The watch should be parallel to the ground.
- Point the hour hand toward the sun.
- Bisect (that means divide in half) the line between the hour hand and the twelve o'clock mark to find south. Measure clockwise from the hour hand to noon if the time is before noon. Measure counterclockwise if it's after noon.
- The point directly opposite south on the watch is—you guessed it!—north.

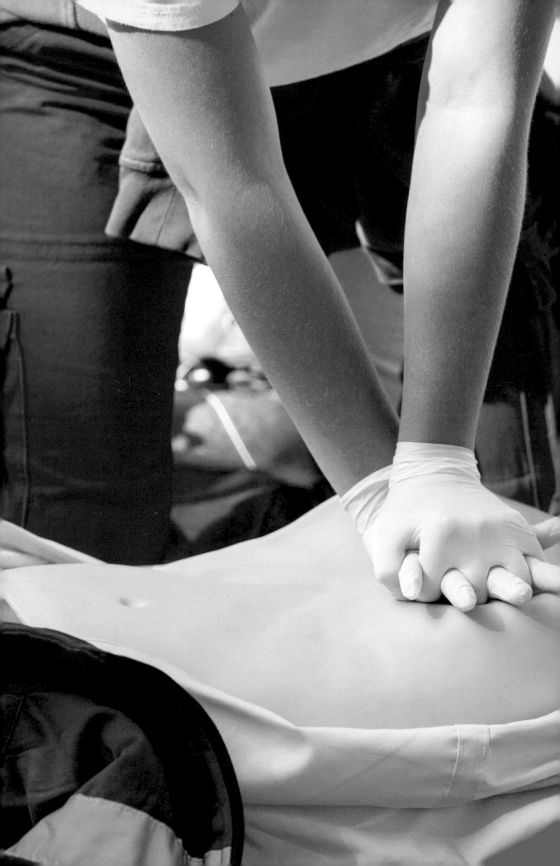

# FIRST AID BASICS

# Build the Perfect First Aid Kit

Accidents and illness can strike at any moment. That's why it's important to be prepared. Every home and car should have a first-aid kit. Here are some essentials to stock up on:

- Bandages of different sizes and shapes
- Sterile gauze pads
- Cloth tape
- A roll of elastic bandages
- Antibiotic ointment or cream
- Hydrocortisone ointment or cream
- Burn ointment or cream
- Antiseptic wipes
- Tweezers
- Pain relievers
- Thermometer
- Scissors
- Allergy medicine
- Instant cold packs
- Non-latex gloves
- A blanket
- Splints
- A one-way mouthpiece (for administering CPR)
- Any medications you or your family require
- A first aid manual

⚠ **SAFETY TIP: Set It, But Don't Forget It**
Be sure to check your first aid kit frequently. Replace any supplies that have been used and review the expiration dates to see if anything needs to be restocked.

# Stop the Bleeding!

Being able to stop bleeding is an important and life-saving skill. Here's what to do if you or someone else gets a big boo-boo:

1. Cover the injury with a gauze pad, bandage, or clean cloth.
2. Press the bandage down on the injury. Keep up the pressure until the bleeding stops.
3. If the blood soaks through, do not remove it. Add another layer and continue to press down.
4. If the injury is on the patient's arm or leg, raise the limb above the heart to slow the bleeding.
5. Seek medical attention as soon as possible.

## Stopping Nosebleeds

1. Have the person sit up and lean forward. They should not tip their head back or the blood will go down their throat. (Yuck!)
2. Pinch the bridge of their nose.
3. Hold a piece of gauze against their nose to soak up the blood.
4. Get to a doctor if the bleeding doesn't stop or the person feels faint.

## When to Call 911

- Bleeding is very heavy.
- Blood is spurting from the wound. (This could indicate an artery has been cut.)
- The injury is on the chest or abdomen.
- You suspect internal bleeding.
- The bleeding doesn't stop after applying pressure for 10 minutes.

# Heart-Stopping: Administering CPR

CPR, or cardiopulmonary resuscitation, can save someone's life. Although CPR is fairly simple to administer, doing so can be a scary experience, so it's best to take a class to become certified. Here are the basic steps:

### I. Check the Scene.
If the victim is in immediate danger—in the middle of the road, for example—move them to safety right away.

### 2. Check for Responsiveness.
Get close to the patient and ask them if they are okay in a loud voice. Tap them on the cheek or shake their shoulder firmly to see if you get a response. If there is no response, check if they are breathing.

### 3. Get Help.
Call 911 immediately, or have a bystander call for you. The dispatcher can talk you through performing CPR and send help at the same time.

### 4. Get in Position.
Place the victim flat on their back. Kneel beside them so you are next to their chest. Place one hand in the center of the victim's chest, with your other hand lying on top of it. Your elbows should be locked, and your shoulders should be directly over your hands.

### 5. Press and Count.

Push down on the victim's chest to a depth of about two inches and let it return to normal position. This is called a chest compression. You want to perform 30 chest compressions, at the rate of about 100-120 beats per minute. Don't worry about doing math. Just think of the popular disco song "Stayin' Alive" by the Bee Gees. Really—it has the perfect beat for CPR. You can also use "Baby Shark."

### 6. Take Two Breaths.

Now it's time for two rescue breaths. Stop pushing and tilt the victim's head back to open their airway. Pinch the nose shut and cover their mouth with your own to create a seal. Breathe into the patient's mouth and watch the chest to make sure it rises. If it doesn't, adjust the head position and try again. Allow the chest to rise and fall between breaths.

### 7. Repeat Until Help Arrives.

After two breaths, go back to chest compressions. Continue to alternate 30 chest compressions and two breaths until paramedics come or the patient starts breathing. Do not let more than ten seconds pass between sets of compressions.

### BABY STEPS

Performing CPR on a small child or a baby is almost the same, but there are a few important differences.

1. For a child, place the heel of one hand on the center of the victim's chest to do compressions.
2. For a baby, use two thumbs to do compressions. Place your thumbs just below their nipples. Wrap your other fingers around the baby's back for support.
3. When doing rescue breaths on a baby, cover BOTH the baby's nose and mouth with your mouth.

### WHAT IF . . . ?

If the patient's chest doesn't rise and fall when you give rescue breaths, there might be something blocking their airway. Place your fingers in their mouth and sweep them from side-to-side to clear away any blockage. Do NOT stick your fingers down their throat—that can push the object deeper. If you cannot get the patient to breathe, just continue doing the chest compressions.

# How to Use an AED

AED stands for automatic external defibrillator. On someone needing CPR, this device can diagnose an irregular heartbeat and provide an appropriate electric shock to jolt the heart back into a normal rhythm. Most AEDs can be used on children and adults who weigh at least 55 pounds.

While using one might sound terrifying, AEDs are programmed to actually teach you what to do, step by step. Here's a quick guide:

### 1. Check and Call.
Make sure the victim is in a safe place where they won't be hurt even more. Check for responsiveness and breathing. Call 911, or have someone else make the call while you take care of the victim.

### 2. Get Ready to Rumble.
Take off all clothing covering the chest. Move any jewelry out of the way as well. If the victim is wet, be sure to dry off their chest.

### 3. Ready, Set, Go!
Turn on the AED and follow the prompts it gives you as closely as you possibly can. It will probably tell you to place one pad on the upper right side of the chest. Place the other pad on the left side, a few inches below the armpit. (If the patient is so small and skinny that the pads are touching, place the second pad on the patient's back between the shoulder blades.)

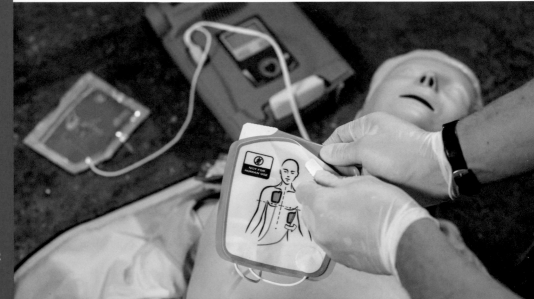

### 4. Check It Out.

Plug the pad connector cable into the AED. Say "Clear!" in a loud voice to prevent anyone from touching the victim. The AED will analyze the heart rhythm.

### 5. Shocking News.

After the AED uses the pads to "read" the current heart rhythm, it will tell you if the victim needs to be shocked. If it does, say "Clear!" again. Do not touch the victim, and make sure no one else does either. Then push the shock button on the AED.

### 6. Carry On.

After the AED delivers the shock, go back to doing CPR until help arrives. You should also continue CPR if the AED indicates no shock is necessary.

> ⚠ **SAFETY TIP: Practice Makes Perfect**
> AEDs can be found in most public buildings and workplaces. It's a good idea to get in the habit of noting the location of these devices when you're out and about—at school, at the grocery store, even at public parks. Most CPR classes include AED training as well—another great reason to take a class. Get practice and you'll be even more prepared for an emergency.

# Allergy Action

An allergy is an extreme reaction of the body's immune system. Whether the cause is a PB&J or a bee sting, an allergic reaction needs to be treated quickly.

Some allergy symptoms are mild, but others can be deadly. Call 911 immediately if the victim has trouble breathing or talking, breaks out in hives, or experiences any swelling of the mouth, tongue, lips, or throat.

## Signs of an Allergic Reaction

- Itchy, watering eyes
- Itchy nose
- Sneezing
- Rashes
- Hives
- Tongue, lip, or face swelling
- Stomach cramps
- Vomiting
- Swelling
- Redness on the skin
- Trouble breathing
- Chest tightness
- Throat closing up
- Wheezing
- Feeling faint

## Common Allergies

- Peanuts
- Tree nuts (like almonds)
- Eggs
- Tree, flower, and grass pollen
- Bee stings
- Insect bites
- Dust
- Animal fur
- Shellfish (shrimp, crab, lobster)
- Some medications

## Minor Reactions

If a person has a mild allergic reaction to something they ate or touched, have them rinse the affected areas with cold water. If their skin is itchy, apply cortisone cream to help. Have the person see a doctor as soon as possible.

## Using an EpiPen

If a person knows they have an allergy, they might carry an EpiPen. This device injects medicine to treat extreme reactions, and they will already know how to use it even if they have never needed to before. But if they physically can't use it on themselves in a crisis, here's what to do:

- Hold the pen in your fist with the blue end facing up (toward the sky).
- Pull off the blue cap.
- Check that the window on the side of the EpiPen is clear.
- Push the pen hard into the victim's thigh. You can inject the EpiPen through clothes, even jeans.
- Listen for a click. Then hold the pen firmly for five seconds while the medicine is injected.
- Remove the EpiPen. An orange cover will slide forward to cover the needle.
- If you haven't already, immediately call 911. Or go to the nearest emergency room.

# Don't Choke!

Choking is one of the scariest first aid situations you can encounter. It's essential to act quickly. Have someone call 911 as you work.

### I. Cough It Out.

If a person is unable to speak or is grabbing their throat or neck, encourage them to cough to remove the obstruction. If that doesn't work, it's time for you to act.

### 2. Smack 'Em Around.

This is one time when you have permission to hit someone. Bend the victim forward and hit them hard in the middle of the back to try to dislodge the obstruction. If you're lucky, you'll see the piece of food or whatever it is fly out of their mouth. Try five firm hits. If that doesn't work, it's time for the next step.

### 3. Do the Abdominal Thrust.

Stand behind the victim and put your arms around their waist. Make one hand into a fist and wrap the other around it, just above their belly button. Press the victim's stomach in and up as hard as you can. This action should force air out of the lungs and into the person's throat, hopefully dislodging what they are choking on.

### When a Baby Chokes?

- Hold the baby along your thigh or forearm with their head down.
- Hit them firmly on the back between the shoulder blades.
- Repeat up to five times until the baby stops choking.
- If the baby is still choking, turn them chest up.

- Place two fingers in the middle of their chest, just below the nipples.
- Push down sharply. Repeat up to five times until the baby stops choking.
- Continue alternating back blows and chest pushes.
- Have someone call 911 as soon as possible.

⚠ **SAFETY TIP: What If You Choke With No One Else Around?**

Call 911 right away, and just stay on the line if you can't talk. Then, give yourself abdominal thrusts to remove the stuck object.

- Place a fist slightly above your belly button.
- Grasp your fist with the other hand.
- Bend over a hard surface, like a desk, counter, or chair.
- Shove your fist inward and upward.

# A Bad Break

If you or someone you're with breaks a bone, treatment depends on which bone is broken. Here are ways to deal with common breaks until you get to a doctor or hospital:

## Splinting an Arm or Leg

A splint keeps an arm or leg from moving and prevents further injury.

1. Wrap the injured limb with a bandage, gauze, or cloth.
2. Place the splint (anything that is stiff, like a stick or folded-over cardboard) on the injured limb. One end should rest on the joint above the break and the other on the joint below it. For example, if you're splinting the lower leg, rest the splint on the knee and the ankle.
3. Use strips of cloth, bandage, or tape to secure the splint to the limb. The splint should be tight but not so tight that it cuts off circulation.

## Splinting Dos and Don'ts

- DO NOT try to push a bone back into place.
- DO check the injury frequently. If it looks pale, blue, or swollen, loosen the splint. An injury often swells, so the splint may be fine when you put it on but become too tight later.
- DO go to the emergency room as soon as possible.

### Splinting a Hand

1. Have the injured person grip something in their hand, like a cloth or a pair of rolled-up socks.
2. Place padding, such as pieces of gauze, between the person's fingers.
3. Wrap the hand securely, covering it from fingertips to the wrist.
4. Keep the fingertips uncovered so you can check for signs of poor circulation. If the fingertips or nails turn blue, loosen the splint.

### How to Make a Sling

If a person has injured their arm, shoulder, or collarbone, a sling is a great way to support the injury and reduce pain.

1. You can make a sling out of any large piece of cloth—a shirt or jacket works too.
2. If you can, cut or fold the cloth into a triangle.
3. Place the person's elbow at one point of the triangle, with the body of the triangle running along the forearm and wrist.
4. Bring the two free points up around the front and back of the shoulder, and tie them securely.
5. Adjust the sling so the arm rests comfortably inside it. The hand should be higher than the elbow, and the elbow should be bent at a right angle. Make sure the arm rests against the person's chest and the fingertips are showing.

> ⚠ **SAFETY TIP: Catch a Break**
> Always remove rings, bracelets, and watches from an injured arm, hand, or leg before applying a splint or sling. As the injury swells, the jewelry can become so tight, it cuts off circulation.

# Sprains and Strains

Instead of hopping around on one foot, take these steps to feel better.

### Sprain vs. Strain: What's the Difference?
**A sprain** occurs when you tear or twist a ligament (that's the tissue that connects the joints).
**A strain** is an overstretched or pulled muscle.
Both injuries can cause swelling, pain, and tenderness.

Sprains are treated with **RICE**. No, not the food. RICE stands for **R**est, **I**ce, **C**ompress, and **E**levate.

- **Rest**. Don't put weight on the injury. It's time to sit down and put your feet up.
- **Ice**. Apply an ice pack for 15-20 minutes. Take a 20-minute break, then apply again. If you don't have a bag of ice, use a bag of frozen vegetables wrapped in a towel.
- **Compress**. Wrap a bandage around the injured limb.
- **Elevate**. Raise the injured limb by placing it on a pillow.

See a doctor if the injury becomes very swollen or continues to hurt a lot after the first day.

# Eye Dos and Eye Don'ts

**If a small object is in the eye:**

- DO NOT rub the eye.
- DO NOT touch the eyeball.
- DO look up and pull down the lower eyelid.
- DO remove the object with the corner of a moist cloth.
- DO cover the eye with a dressing.

**If the eye is cut:**

- DO cover the eye with a paper cup and a bandage.
- DO keep the eye as still as possible.
- DO get medical attention right away.

**If the eye is injured from a punch or other blow:**

- DO place an ice pack over the eye and surrounding area.
- DO NOT place a steak on your eye! This only works in cartoons.
- DO visit the doctor as soon as you can.

**If a large object is in the eye:**

- DON'T try to remove an object that has penetrated the eye.
- DO cover the eye with a paper cup or place pads above and below the eye.
- DO NOT touch the eye or allow the pads or cup to touch it.
- DO go to the hospital right away.

**If the eye is burned or comes in contact with a chemical:**

- DO rinse the eye with cold water for 20 minutes.
- DO place a light bandage over the eye.
- DO find out what the chemical was.
- DO go to the hospital right away.

# Hot, Hot, Hot!

Burns can be really painful. Here's how to tell minor burns from severe ones, and what to do.

## It's All About Degrees.

- A **first-degree burn** only affects the top layer of skin. The skin may be red and painful.
- A **second-degree burn** affects two layers of skin. They cause pain, redness, swelling, and blistering.
- A **third-degree burn** is very serious because it burns all layers of skin. The skin turns white or black and may feel numb. Third-degree burns ALWAYS require immediate medical attention. Call 911 or go to the hospital right away!

⚠ **SAFETY TIP: Not All Sunscreen Is Created Equal**
Sprays, lotions, and sticks—oh my! Sunscreen comes in so many varieties it's hard to know which to use. Pick a broad-spectrum sunscreen (this means the label should say it protects against UVA and UVB rays). Think about what you'll be doing and whether you need it to be water resistant. Look for an SPF of at least 30 that has zinc oxide or titanium dioxide as one of its ingredients. And then make sure to reapply every one or two hours in the sun—even more if you're in the water.

## Treating Minor Burns

- Remove any jewelry right away, before the injury swells.
- Rinse minor burns under cool (not cold!) water for about 10 minutes.
- If the burn can't be rinsed easily, apply a cold compress or ice pack.
- Apply a moisturizing lotion or burn ointment or cream.
- Cover with a loose bandage. Be sure the bandage doesn't rub against the skin.
- DO NOT break any blisters. If a blister does pop, apply antibiotic cream or ointment and a bandage.
- If a person has second-degree burns over a large area of their body, call 911 or go to the hospital right away.

## Treating Sunburn

- Cool the skin by placing a cold, wet washcloth over the burned area. Or take a cool bath or shower.
- Apply moisturizing lotion. Lotions that contain aloe vera or calamine are especially helpful.
- Place the bottle of lotion in the refrigerator before you apply it to make it even more soothing.
- Drink extra water.
- Don't pop blisters or peel off burned skin.
- Sunburns can be itchy when they heal, but try not to scratch! You'll irritate and tear the skin, and you can even cause an infection.

# More Than a Bump on the Head

While most bumps and bruises heal on their own, a serious head injury can cause a concussion or even a traumatic brain injury.

### Spotting a Concussion

A concussion occurs when a blow or other injury causes the head and brain to move violently back and forth. Symptoms of a concussion include:

- Headache
- Dizziness
- Nausea
- Vomiting
- Ringing in the ears

- Drowsiness
- Blurred vision
- Confusion
- Trouble speaking
- Loss of memory

### Treating a Concussion

Get checked out by a doctor if you have any symptoms of a concussion or if you receive a hard blow to the head. You'll probably be advised to take over-the-counter pain relievers, rest your eyes, and avoid looking at screens for a few days or weeks. You won't be allowed to take part in sports for a while either.

Most concussions heal within a few weeks, but some effects last longer. If you're not back to normal or your symptoms get worse, see a doctor right away.

## Other Head Injuries

Here are some tips to deal with head injuries:

- Call 911 right away.
- Control any bleeding.
- Tell the patient to lie still and not move their head or neck.
- If there is an open wound, cover it with a clean cloth or bandage. Do not try to clean the wound or explore it with your fingers.
- Do not press on the injury.
- If the patient is going to vomit, roll them onto their side while supporting their head, neck, and back so they do not choke.

> ⚠ **SAFETY TIP: Better Safe Than Sorry**
> Call 911 right away if a person with a head injury loses consciousness, stops breathing, seems confused, can't move a body part, can't speak clearly, or has different-sized pupils. If something is seriously wrong, the best bet is to have them checked out by medical professionals as soon as possible.

# Stroke

A stroke happens when the brain loses oxygen. This usually occurs because a blood vessel bursts or is clogged up. Strokes are very serious and must be treated right away.

You can recognize signs of a stroke by thinking FAST:

- **Face Drooping:** One side of the patient's face will be lower than the other. If you ask the person to smile, they may only move one corner of their mouth.
- **Arm Weakness:** One arm feels numb or weak. Ask the person to lift both arms and see if they can raise both to the same height.
- **Speech Weakness:** The person may not be able to speak or may slur their words or say things that don't make sense.
- **Time to Call 911:** Call right away! Note what time the symptoms first appeared.

While you're waiting for medical help, keep the patient calm and quiet. Talk to them reassuringly and let them know that help is on the way. Encourage them to sit or lie down. Don't let them fall asleep, and don't give them anything to eat or drink, including any medicine. Stay close by until help arrives.

# I'm Shocked!

You might feel shocked when you hear unexpected news, but shock is also a medical condition—and it's a serious one. Shock happens when a person is injured, and their blood doesn't flow to their organs the way it should.

## Signs of Shock

- Low blood pressure
- Rapid heartbeat
- Shallow breathing
- Feeling very tired
- Feeling anxious
- Dizziness
- Confusion
- Sweating
- Pale, cool, or clammy skin

## Treating Shock

- Call 911 immediately.
- Make sure the victim is lying down.
- Elevate feet about 12 inches.
- Cover them with a blanket.
- Monitor their breathing.

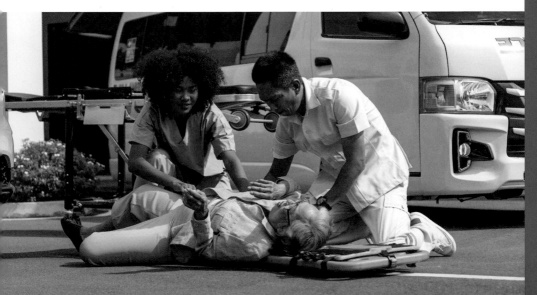

# Just Breathe

Most of us can get enough oxygen without even thinking about it. But during an asthma attack, the airways narrow, making breathing difficult. If you or someone nearby appears to be having an asthma attack, here's what to do.

## Asthma Assistant

- Help the person having the attack sit in a comfortable position and help them get their inhaler. This may mean sending someone else for it, if it's across the room or in a backpack stashed nearby.
- Meanwhile, help them to sit up and lean forward slightly. This may make it easier for them to breathe. Encourage them to breathe slowly and deeply.
- When the inhaler is available, stay nearby in case they need any help while they use it. They probably know exactly what to do.

## When to Call 911 for an Asthma Attack

Some people have asthma attacks a lot and don't need medical attention every time. Call 911 if . . .

- They are having their first attack.
- They stop breathing.
- They are finding it difficult to talk or even make a noise.
- They aren't helped by their inhaler.
- They don't have any asthma medication with them.
- They get worse.

# Seizure Sense

Seizures can look very scary, but they usually don't cause the person having them pain or discomfort. A seizure can occur because of a medical condition, such as epilepsy, or as a result of an injury or illness. If someone has a seizure, keep your cool and follow these steps:

- Make sure the person is not in danger. Move them to a safe place, such as out of the road or away from stairs, sharp objects, or furniture.
- Lower the person to the ground.
- Do not try to restrain the person or hold them down.
- Do not put anything—including your fingers—into the person's mouth.
- Time the seizure with the stopwatch on your phone.
- After the seizure ends, the person may be confused or sleepy. Stay with them as they recover.
- If the seizure lasts more than five minutes, causes an injury, or is followed by another seizure, call 911.

# ANIMAL
# ATTACKS

# What to Do If You Run Into a Shark

You're happily splashing around in the ocean, when suddenly you see a shadow in the water. A fin breaks the surface. It's a shark! And you just might be shark bait!

First, some facts. Shark attacks get a lot of attention, but in fact they are very rare. There are over 500 species of sharks in the world. Of those, only a dozen are considered dangerous to humans. So the odds of a shark taking a bite out of you are pretty slim.

**Second fact:** Shark attacks are usually a case of mistaken identity. Sharks don't really want to eat people. What they hunger for are seals. Unfortunately, a person swimming can look a lot like a seal. So it's no wonder a shark can get confused.

In the unlikely event that a shark is coming for you, here's how to survive:

## I. Play It Safe.

Most shark attacks happen at night, or at dawn and dusk. You're a lot safer swimming in broad daylight. Sharks also like to hang out around sand bars or in places where the water depth changes quickly. And it's not a good idea to swim in areas also used for sport fishing, as the water will be full of bait that could attract sharks. Oh, and swimming on a beach that has lifeguards is always a good idea. Of course, you should NEVER swim on a beach that has been closed because of shark activity, not even if someone dares you.

### 2. Buddy Up.

Swimming with a buddy is always a good idea when you're in the water, and it can prevent shark attacks. Why? Sharks are more likely to attack a lone swimmer than a pair or group. There is safety in numbers!

### 3. Bad Attraction.

Sharks are attracted to certain things. One of them is shiny things. Sparkly jewelry or bathing suits can look like fish scales, and that can make a hungry shark get closer. Sharks may or may not be attracted to fresh blood. Scientists aren't sure about that, but it's best to stay out of the water if you are bleeding.

### 4. Don't Panic!

What if a shark gets too close? Stay calm! Sharks are attracted to splashing, especially if they already think you're a tasty seal. So splashing and thrashing around out of panic is the worst thing you can do. Instead, be as still as you can. Odds are, the shark is just curious and will swim away once it figures out you are not a seal. If it doesn't, move backwards, ideally toward shore, always keeping the shark in sight, and swim away slowly.

### 5. Let 'Em Have It!

If the worst happens and a shark does attack, it's time to fight back. Make like an MMA fighter and kick, punch, and hit. Soft spots, like the gills or eyes, are good places to aim for. If you have an object at hand, like a snorkel mask, a surfboard, or a camera, whack the beast with that too.

### 6. Yell for Help.

Let people know you're in danger. Yell, scream, wave your arms! If a lifeguard, other swimmers, or someone on a nearby boat realizes you're in trouble, they can help you out— and maybe even save your life.

# Lions and Bears, Oh My!

You might be on a camping trip or just taking a walk in the woods when suddenly you see a mountain lion or a bear headed your way. Here's what to do to stay alive.

- Preventing an attack is the best way to stay safe. Walk with a group and make a lot of noise: Sing, talk, anything that will let a predator know you're there. Odds are, they will want to avoid you just as much as you want to avoid them.
- If you see a mountain lion or a bear before it sees you, make a quick, quiet getaway. Move away slowly and calmly. Don't try to get closer to take a selfie!
- If the mountain lion or bear is coming toward you, think big! Make yourself look as big as possible—spread out your arms, or hold up your jacket or sweatshirt. NEVER bend down—it makes you look small and defenseless, and also more like a prey animal.
- If the lion or bear continues to approach, yell and throw something at it. Anything will do—a water bottle, rocks, sticks, whatever you can grab!
- Have a backpack? Swing it around to scare the animal off. If the animal keeps coming, strap the pack across the front of your body to protect your core.
- Never turn your back on a predator. Instead, back away slowly and maintain eye contact. Don't run—that will just make the lion or bear chase you!

⚠ **SAFETY TIP: Bear in Mind!**
Bears like food. To keep bears away from your home or campsite, never leave food outside. Don't leave food trash around either. Don't keep food in your tent—a bear could break in! Instead, hang it in a sturdy bag at least 10 feet off the ground. At home, don't leave pet food outside, and use bear-proof containers for your trash.

# Mind Your Moose Manners

Moose are big—make that huge!—animals with big—also huge!—antlers. Although these animals are usually shy, they can turn into terrifying and dangerous animals if you get too close. To stay safe, follow these tips:

- Moose are usually active at dusk, and they often gather in wet areas, like marshes or near waterways. Try to avoid these places if you can. If you can't, be aware that a moose might be right around the next tree.
- Watch the moose's body language. If it raises the hair on its back and lays back its ears, those are not good signs. If the moose starts walking toward you, it's time to get defensive.
- Back away slowly as the moose approaches. If there is a tree, big rock, or nearby building or vehicle, take shelter behind it.
- Sometimes moose charge, then stop. They are bluffing and trying to scare you away. Continue walking backward slowly toward safety.
- If the worst happens and the moose charges you, run! You might be able to outrun a moose, and the moose will often give up the chase pretty quickly.
- Do you carry bear spray or pepper spray? Use it!
- If the moose keeps coming and you can't run to safety, drop to the ground and curl up in a ball. Protect your head and face with your arms. Don't get up until the moose goes away, or it might come back for more.

# Raging Bull!

If you live in farm country or visit a rural area, you may run into a big, snorting, angry problem! Here are some guidelines.

### I. Stay Away!

Bulls are aggressive, and it doesn't take much to set them off. So the best way to avoid a charging bull is to stay away. That means do not go into a field or enclosure where a bull is hanging out.

### 2. Keep It Down.

If you absolutely must get near a bull or a herd of cows, keep quiet. Try to be invisible. Stay as far away as possible, and don't try to touch them. Leave as quickly and calmly as you can.

### 3. Look for Warning Signs.

If the bull does any of these things, stay as far away as you can (but DON'T run!):

- Shakes his head
- Stares at you
- Lowers his head and paws the dirt
- Breathes loudly or makes a grunting sign

### 4. Stay Calm and Carry a Big Stick.

Sudden movements can make bulls even angrier. Keep calm, and back away slowly. If you can grab a big stick or other object, do so.

### 5. Run for It!

If the bull charges at you, it's time to run! Run in a zigzag pattern, and yell for help. Take off your backpack, sweatshirt, or jacket and throw it at the bull to distract it. Head for a fence or some trees to get anything between you and the charging animal.

### 6. Time to Fight.

If you can't outrun the bull, it's time to fight. Hit the bull as hard as you can on the muzzle or nose. (Don't worry, you won't hurt it.) Yell as loud as you can. Do NOT drop to the ground and "play dead." The bull may continue to attack you if you do.

# Stinky Skunks

These nighttime prowlers have a built-in defense system, and wow, does it stink! Here's the best way to stay odor-free.

### I. Night Time Is the Right Time.

If you see a skunk during the day, or one that is staggering, or acting aggressive or just weird, get inside and call the police. The skunk may have rabies, and it needs to be removed by professionals.

### 2. Doggie Danger.

Do you walk your dogs at night or let them out for a last bathroom break before bedtime? Watch out! Dogs may run up to a skunk and scare it. And then comes the spray.

### 3. Warning Signs.

If the skunk raises its tail, turns its butt toward you, or stomps its feet, run for your life! It is about to spray.

### GOT SKUNKED?

Here's what to do if you or your pet gets sprayed by a skunk:

I. Mix together:
   A. 1 quart of 3% hydrogen peroxide
   B. ¼ cup baking soda
   C. 1 teaspoon liquid dishwashing soap
2. Wearing rubber gloves, wash with this solution. Rub the mixture all over and scrub deep to get rid of the stench.
3. If you're washing your dog or cat, don't leave the mixture on longer than you have to, because peroxide can bleach fur.
4. Rinse thoroughly. The worst of the smell should be gone.

DO NOT get the solution in your eyes—or your pet's.
DO NOT store this mixture or make it ahead of time, as the mixture could explode if left in a bottle.

# What to Do About Venomous Animals

You've probably seen a snake attack in a movie or TV show. There's an urgent rush to get medical attention before it's too late. In real life, medical attention is exactly what you need. And there are more venomous animals than snakes to worry about!

### Snakes Alive!

There are several venomous snakes in the United States. The rattlesnake is probably the best known. Copperheads, cottonmouths, and coral snakes are venomous too. To avoid getting bitten by one of these bad boys, take the following steps:

- Know where snakes are likely to be. Long grass, piles of leaves, fallen logs, and under rocks are all great hiding places.
- Carry a big stick. Use it to sweep through long grass to scare away snakes.
- Watch your walk. Stay on clear paths, if possible. Look before you step. If you're rock climbing, try to peek before you reach your hand out. A snake just may be sunbathing there!
- Carry a flashlight if you're walking at night.
- Dress for success. Wear long pants and shoes or boots that cover your ankles and have thick soles.
- Find a dead snake? Don't touch! Some snakes can bite out of a reflex after death.

If you're bitten by a venomous snake:

- Dial 911 or send someone for help IMMEDIATELY! You'll probably need a trip to the hospital for a dose of antivenom, and you need to get there fast! Meanwhile:
- Remember what the snake looks like.
- Take off any jewelry or clothing near the bite, because your body may swell up fast.

- Wash out the wound, wiping away from the bite.
- Place the bitten limb level with or below your heart.
- DO NOT cut the wound or try to suck out the venom.

### Lizard Bites

Luckily, there's only one venomous lizard in the United States, and that's the Gila monster. These critters hang out in the desert. Unluckily, a Gila's monster's bite is extremely painful. These liz-  ards will actually chew on the bite to release more venom! Gila monster venom is usually not enough to kill a human. Still, getting bitten is no fun, and you will need medical help.

If you see a Gila monster, back away and leave it alone. If it hisses at you, get away fast! Hissing means a lizard is about to bite.

If the lizard does bite you, lower its feet to the ground to encourage it to let go. Or use a small stick to pry its jaws open.

Place the bitten limb below your heart. Call 911 and get help right away.

### Scary Spiders

Say hello to the black widow, the brown widow, and the brown recluse. On second thought, say goodbye! These three venomous spiders live in the United States, and you don't want to meet them.

All three like to hang out in warm, dry places. A pile of wood, the inside of a shed, or an attic or basement are all ideal for these spiders. So it's best to be careful around these areas, and always be on the lookout.

Brown widow and brown recluse spider bites are very painful, but they probably won't kill you. However, you will feel very sick. If you are bitten, call 911. A black widow spider's venom, on the other hand, can be almost 15 times stronger than a rattlesnake's! You'll need to go straight to the emergency room.

No matter what kind of spider bites you, wash the bite with soap and water, and put ice on it to reduce swelling. It's also a good idea to elevate the bitten area.

# Watch Out for Killer Bees!

Yes, there actually are killer bees. Their real name is Africanized Killer Bees, and they were created when bees from Africa mated with honeybees in Brazil. The result was a big, aggressive bee that is always in a bad mood. These bees spread northward through South and Central America and eventually reached parts of the United States. They have been known to swarm in large numbers and chase victims for more than a quarter mile.

Killer bees are not found everywhere, but other bees, along with wasps, yellow jackets, and hornets, can also be scary, especially if you may be allergic. Here are a few Dos and Don'ts:

- DO look around. If you see more than one, there may be a nest or hive nearby, and the best thing to do is walk away.
- DO watch where you walk. Some hornets and bees nest in the ground.
- DO run for it. Killer bees will chase you, but as soon as you're away from their hive, they are likely to stop
- DON'T swat at bees or wasps.
- DON'T leave sweet food or drinks uncovered or open. Bees love sugar.

If you get stung:

- DO try to remove the stinger. Scrape the area with your fingernail or the edge of a credit card.
- DON'T squeeze or poke at the stinger. That could release more venom.
- DON'T scratch!
- DO wash the area with soap and water.
- DO apply ice or a cold washcloth to reduce swelling.
- DO take an antihistamine (with a parent's help). You can also apply hydrocortisone cream to reduce pain and itching.
- DO call 911 right away if you have trouble breathing, your throat or mouth swells, or you feel weak or sick. You could be having an allergic reaction.

# Crikey! It's a Croc (Or an Alligator)!

What does a crocodile or an alligator eat for lunch? Anything it wants to—and that might include you! These rowdy reptiles are what's called super predators. That means they are powerful enough to attack any animal—or human—that gets too close. Here's how to avoid being on the menu.

- Crocodiles and alligators like water, and they often live near swamps and marshes. Keep a lookout when you are in these areas. And if you see a "Warning" or "No Swimming" sign, don't go in or near the water!
- Gators and crocs are great swimmers. They move fast—up to 20 miles (32 kilometers) an hour! You can't outswim one, so it's best to stay away.
- Alligators and crocodiles aren't so good at running, thanks to their short legs. So if you're faced with a hungry creature, run away as fast as you can! Pro tip: Run in a straight line. You'll get away faster.

- These creatures do what's called a "death roll" when they catch their prey in the water. They roll over and hold their prey under the water until it drowns. So if a gator or croc grabs you, roll up into a ball so it's harder for the animal to roll with you. If that doesn't work, fight back by punching, kicking, and poking at its eyes.
- ALWAYS go to a hospital after a croc or gator attack, even if you only got a flesh wound. These reptiles have loads of nasty bacteria in their mouths, and an untreated wound can get infected. Yuck!

### Alligator or Crocodile?

How can you tell the difference between an alligator and a crocodile? Look at their heads! Alligators have wide, rounded snouts. Crocodiles have narrow, pointy snouts. Some of a crocodile's teeth stick out when its mouth is closed, but an alligator's teeth do not.

# Who Let the Dogs Out?

Dogs can be great friends and companions. But some dogs don't want to be petted by you—and they may even bite you! Dog attacks can be very dangerous. Here's how to avoid them.

- DO careful around dogs you don't know.
- DON'T try to touch or pet a strange dog, even if it's on a leash.
- DO ask the dog's owner for permission first. Always. If they say no, there's probably a good reason.
- DO pay attention to a dog's body language. If its head is up and its tail is wagging, that's a good sign. If it's hunched over, or growling and baring its teeth, and its tail is down, it's time to back off.
- DO let the dog come to you. Let them sniff you if they want.
- DON'T stick your hand in a dog's face. You wouldn't like it if a stranger did that to you, would you?
- DO be careful approaching a loose dog or a pack of dogs. They may be aggressive or just scared. Either way, things could get ugly fast.
- DO carry dog protection products, such as citronella spray. Some people even carry small air horns to scare away aggressive dogs!
- DO "Be a Tree." That means you should stand still with your arms at your sides and your hands folded in front of you. Keep your head down and don't stare at the dog.

## Attack!

What if you meet an aggressive dog? The key is to keep calm. If you run, scream, kick, or wave your arms, you're just likely to make the dog feel more threatened—and more aggressive. Better to stand slightly sideways and not make direct eye contact. Hopefully, the dog will realize you aren't a threat and go away.

If that doesn't work, try to keep space between you and the dog. If you're carrying a backpack or an umbrella, hold it out in front of you. That will force the dog back and also protect your body.

Worst case scenario: The dog bites you. If the dog sinks its teeth into your jacket or sweater, try to pull the clothing off so it gets a mouthful of fabric instead of flesh. Cover your face and tuck in your fingers to protect them. Yell for help.

This sounds weird, but if a dog bites your arm or hand, don't try to pull it away. That will only make the dog bite down harder. Instead, push the body part deeper into the dog's mouth. Often, the dog will let go. You can also try lifting the dog's back legs into the air to make it want to let go. Crazy, but true!

After the attack is over, be sure to get medical attention. Your injuries could get infected. If the owner is there, get their contact info.

Dogs can carry rabies and its owner will have to show a vaccination certificate, to make sure it's healthy. If not, you may need rabies shots to stay healthy yourself.

# DANGEROUS
# SITUATIONS

# How to Survive a Plane Crash

It's terrifying to think about. But in 2020, there were 24.4 million plane flights and just 40 accidents. The odds of being killed in a plane crash are teeny-tiny. Still, being prepared is exactly what can help you survive the unlikely—and unlucky—event.

### 1. Look Around.

As soon as you get in your seat, look around. Where is the nearest emergency exit? Remember, it might be behind you or across the aisle. Count how many rows separate you from it.

### 2. What to Wear.

Wearing a long-sleeved shirt and long pants can protect your skin from fire or flying debris in case of a crash. It's also important to wear sturdy shoes. It's hard to escape wearing flip-flops or high heels, so pack those in your luggage instead.

### 3. Pay Attention!

All flights start with a safety demonstration or video. Even if this is your 100th flight, pay attention! Not every plane is the same, and safety devices might be stored somewhere you didn't expect.

### 4. Remember the Three and Eight Rule.

Most crashes happen during takeoff (the first three minutes of a flight) or landing (the last eight minutes). Make sure your seat belt is fastened, your shoes are on, and you are not sleeping or eating.

> ⚠ **SAFETY TIP: Does Your Seat Matter?**
> Is there such a thing as a safe seat on a plane? The answer is no . . . and yes. Because not all plane crashes are the same, it's impossible to choose one area that is always safe. However, studies have shown that it is a bit safer to sit in a middle seat in the rear of the plane.

Okay, the worst has happened, and your plane is going down. You can still increase your chances of walking away by following these simple rules.

### I. Listen to Your Flight Crew.
Flight attendants are trained to keep you safe—it's the most important part of their job. Listen to them and follow their instructions. They know what they're talking about.

### 2. Get Comfy.
No, we don't mean snuggle in and take a nap. We mean padding! Cushion your body with whatever you can find—a pillow, your backpack, your jacket, whatever! Extra padding can be great protection in a crash.

### 3. Brace, Brace, Brace.
If your flight crew tells you to brace, do it! Bracing has been shown to dramatically increase a person's chance of survival. To brace, place your feet flat on the floor and the backs of your hands against the back of the seat in front of you. Then lean forward and rest your forehead on your palms. If this is not possible, tuck your head down and wrap your arms around your knees.

### 4. Get Out!
As soon as the plane stops moving, get out as fast as you can. Leave your personal belongings behind. Find the nearest exit or any opening in the plane (but look before you leap!). If the crew tells you to use the emergency slide, follow their instructions. Most of all, DON'T PANIC! Move away from the aircraft and wait for help.

# How to Survive a Car Crash

Car crashes are scary—maybe because they can happen at any time, even to safe drivers. Sadly, about 46,000 people die in car accidents every year. However, most car crashes are minor. Here are some things you can do to stay safe and unhurt in a crash.

- Wear your seat belt! It's not just the law, it's the best way to protect yourself. Without a seat belt, the impact of a crash can send you flying.
- Cut down on car clutter. Any loose object inside a car can become a missile in a crash. So clean out all those food containers and half-full water bottles!
- Sit up straight. This allows the car's seats and seat belts to protect you in a crash.
- Car windows are hard to break, but you can keep a special device for just that in your car for an emergency. Having one could make escape much easier!
- If a crash does occur, get out of the vehicle as soon as you can (but watch out for other hazards, such as oncoming traffic). Help anyone who is injured. And call 911.

## Water Landings

Just the thought of crashing into a body of water is enough to give you nightmares. If this happens to you, the best thing to do is stay calm. Open your windows as fast as you can. Yes, this lets more water into the car, but it also creates an escape route. You won't be able to open the car door underwater, especially if the doors are locked. Help others in the car identify an escape route too. Then, take a deep breath, and swim for the surface.

# How to Survive a Train Crash

Taking a train is one of the safest ways to travel. But crashes do happen. Here's how to get out alive:

- Choose a safe seat. The front cars of a train are most likely to be damaged in a crash. Instead, choose a car that's two or three cars from the front. And find a backward-facing seat if you can.
- The conductor may warn passengers if a crash is about to happen. Listen to any announcements and follow instructions. Screaming and panicking are NOT going to help.
- If you have time, brace yourself by planting your feet firmly on the floor, leaning forward, and covering your head with your hands. Or place your hands on the back of the seat in front of you and rest your head on them.
- After the crash, escape as soon as you can. Remember, most train windows can be pushed outward in case of emergency.
- Help others and follow directions from train crew members.

# Fire!

No lie, a house fire is one of the scariest things a person can experience. You may have less than two minutes to escape. Here are some top tips:

### I. Alarm Yourself.
Every home should have smoke detectors. There should be at least one on every floor, including sleeping areas. Test smoke detectors every month and change the batteries twice a year.

### 2. Make a Plan.
It's family meeting time! Walk through your home and identify at least two escape routes in every room. Plan different scenarios. For example, if the front door is blocked, do you know how to open the window wide enough to escape that way? It's also important to pick a place outside where the family can meet safely. Even the littlest kids should know what to do—and not do—when the smoke alarm sounds.

### 3. Equip Yourself.
Every home should have at least one fire extinguisher, and everyone should know how to use it.

### 4. Stay Low.

Heat rises, and so will most of a fire's smoke and dangerous fumes. When escaping a fire, crawl along the floor. Pull your shirt over your mouth and nose to block fumes.

### 5. Feel for Flames.

Before you open a door, feel it with the back of your hand. If it's hot, that means there's fire on the other side. Use your second escape route to get out.

### 6. Stop, Drop, and Roll.

If you or your clothes catch fire, don't panic and don't run! Instead, STOP moving, DROP to the ground, and ROLL to put out the fire.

### 7. Don't Look Back.

Once you've escaped, do not go back inside for any reason. Your possessions are not worth more than your life.

### 8. Call for Help.

Once you're safely outside, call 911.

### If You're Trapped Inside . . .

- Call 911 if possible. Try to describe exactly where you are.
- Cover the cracks in the door with anything you can find: blankets, towels, clothes, etc. Bonus points if you can wet the item before you stuff it around the door.
- Cover your mouth and nose to protect them from smoke. Again, it will help if you can wet the covering.
- Hang a blanket or other item outside the window to signal rescuers that you're trapped.
- Wait for help. Do not attempt to run through flames.

# Fires in Public Places

What if a fire breaks out while you're at school, the movies, or some other public place?

- Always be aware of where the exits are.
- Alert others around you by yelling "Fire" if you are the first to see flames.
- If a fire alarm goes off, exit the building in an orderly way.
- Always assume a fire alarm going off means a real fire, not a drill.
- Do not stop to take the time to collect your things. Getting out of the building safely is your first concern.
- Do not run, scream, shove, or panic.
- Use stairs if you're not on a ground floor. It is not safe to use elevators in a fire.
- Follow directions from teachers, staff, or firefighters. Listen for announcements and do what they say.
- Call 911.

# Crowd Crush!

Picture this: You're at a concert having a great time. Bodies are packed tightly around you. Suddenly, everyone pushes forward. You trip and start to fall. It's hard to breathe. You're trapped in a crowd crush! Here's what to do.

### I. Be Aware.
As soon as you get in any crowd, look around. Where are the nearest exits or escape routes? Look for any barriers in your way, such as a wall, a fence, or equipment, and plan how to get around it. Stay away from narrow spaces.

### 2. Take a Step Back.
If you feel too much pressure from the crowd, try to get away from the center of the crowd. You'll be safer and have more space on the edges.

### 3. Stay on Your Feet.
Falling in a crowd is dangerous. If the crowd is moving as one, pick up your feet and ride with its motion instead of trying to stand still or push back. Keep your hands at chest level and your elbows out to protect your body and keep room around yourself and your lungs.

### 4. Save Your Breath.
Don't scream or panic. That just wastes precious oxygen. Instead, breathe normally and stay calm.

### 5. Curl Up.
If you do fall, curl into a ball and cover your face with your arms.

# Help! I'm Drowning!

No one wants a day on the water to turn into tragedy. Here are some ways to stay safe around water!

- Learn to swim. Even basic swimming lessons can help you.
- Don't swim alone. There should always be someone nearby, just in case.
- Don't swim in off-limits areas, or areas where there is no lifeguard.
- Never jump into water without knowing what's under the surface. There might be obstacles you can't see, or the water might not be as deep as you thought.
- On a boat? Always wear a life jacket.
- Never leave a child unsupervised around water.

⚠ **SAFETY TIP: In Over Your Head**

In cartoons or TV shows, drowning victims often yell and wave their arms. In real life, that doesn't happen. Drowning victims often sink under the surface and can't shout for help. They may be in an upright position and moving their arms up and down. If you see this, help the person ASAP. But be careful trying to rescue someone. Drowning makes people panic, and your victim may accidentally push you under the surface! Instead, toss them a rope, spare life vest, or a flotation device, or extend a branch or something they can grab onto.

If the worst happens and you find yourself losing control in the water, here's what to do:

- Stay calm. Breathe normally. Don't hold your breath.
- Get rid of anything that weighs you down, such as shoes, jackets, or backpacks.
- FLOAT! Roll onto your back and float. Stay as relaxed as possible.
- Tilt your head backward. Doing this will keep water out of your mouth. It will also cause your legs to move up in the water, which will help you float.
- If you can, kick and paddle toward shore or shallow water.
- Call for help, or raise your arms to signal others if you can.

# What to Do If You're Being Followed . . . Or Worse

Ever get the feeling you're being watched...or followed? Here's how to stay safe in a creepy situation:

## 1. Keep Calm.
Panicking or running could make things worse. Keep walking at a steady pace, while being aware of your surroundings.

## 2. Head for a Crowd.
Walk toward a busy street or go inside a store. Don't be shy about asking a clerk or security guard for help.

## 3. Get Professional Help.
Keep the local police department's number in your phone contacts. You can call them as you walk, tell them your location, and ask for help.

### If the danger escalates:

- Scream, punch, kick, hit, scratch, whatever it takes to cause a scene that might be noticed.
- If you are abducted, stay calm. Pay attention to your surroundings and try to track where the abductor is taking you. For example, count how many turns the car makes, or look for street signs and familiar landmarks or buildings. Listen for sounds, too.
- If you can use your phone, call 911. Even if you can't talk, your location can be tracked.

# How to Survive a Nuclear Attack

No one wants to think about nuclear bombs, but we live in a scary world. And accidents can happen at nuclear plants. If your area faces a nuclear event, here are some tips:

- If you receive a warning that a nuclear attack is coming, you won't have much time to prepare. Seek shelter inside to protect yourself from radiation, or nuclear fallout. Concrete buildings are the best shelter. Basements are good, too. Plan to stay inside for 24 hours up to one week.
- Stay away from windows. Close your eyes and cover your ears, but keep your mouth open to equalize pressure from a blast. Crouch down with your head covered and your arms and legs tucked close to protect them from flying glass or debris.
- If you must go outside in the week after a blast, cover your mouth and nose with a damp cloth. Get inside as soon as possible.
- If you've been exposed, shower with warm water and soap to remove any radiation from your skin. Wipe your nose, eyes, and ears too. Wash all your clothes and seal them in a plastic bag.
- Packaged food, or food that was in your refrigerator or pantry, is safe to eat, but don't eat uncovered food or anything grown outside in the garden.
- Listen to local news for instructions on what to do. The internet and your phone may not work, but battery-powered or hand-cranked radios should be reliable.

## POLICE LINE DO NOT CROSS    POLIC

# Staying Safe Around Guns

Let's get this straight. Guns are not toys. Guns are weapons. Guns are dangerous. Here's how to stay safe around guns and in situations where guns are present.

### Let's NOT Play with Guns

So you're at a friend's house and he takes out a gun to show you. Or you go to someone's house and spot a gun on the table. What should you do?

- Tell your friend you don't play with guns.
- Don't touch the gun, even if you think it might be a toy.
- Don't listen if the friend says the gun is unloaded or safe to handle.
- Always assume a gun is loaded and the safety lock is off.
- Get away from the gun as quickly and calmly as you can.
- If you're at someone's house and don't feel safe, make an excuse and go home.

### Active Shooter Situations

Active shooter events can happen anywhere—at school, in a public place, at a party. While you shouldn't live in fear, it's best to be aware and know what to do in case violence breaks out.

### Active Shooter at School

- Remember: Run, Hide, Fight. That's shorthand for: Run away from the situation by leaving; Hide in a safe place, such as a locked classroom; Fight to save your life, if you have no other choice.

- Follow directions from school staff. They have been trained for these situations.
- If you have to hide, be quiet. No talking, crying, or using a cell phone.
- Don't come out of hiding until law enforcement tells you to. Then, follow their instructions.
- What if you have to fight? There's safety in numbers, so try to stay in a group. Throw things at your attacker. Even setting off a fire sprinkler could work!

## Active Shooter in Public

If you are in an active shooter situation in a store, at the movies, or in another public place:

- Be alert. Always know how you would escape BEFORE anything bad happens.
- Call 911 and describe where you are and what is happening.
- Make a break for the emergency exit.
- Run in a zigzag pattern, not a straight line. A moving target is harder to hit.
- Stay out of public restrooms. There's usually only one way out.
- If you have to hide, make yourself as small and quiet as possible.
- Wait for law enforcement to arrive and follow their instructions.
- Help others who are injured or frightened.

# Lost at Sea

Maybe the motor of your boat conks out, or a bad storm swamps your vessel. Here are some tips to change your situation from lost to found.

### 1. Send a Mayday Call.
Use your ship's radio to call for help right away. Tell rescuers where you are and what happened.

### 2. Gather Supplies.
You never know what you might need. Take inventory of all the supplies on your boat and store them safely. Place food in bags to keep it dry. If you can tie everything down, do so. You don't want a rogue wave to wash away something you really need.

### 3. Save Water.
Oh, the irony. You're surrounded by water, but you can't drink any of it. (Really. Don't.) Resist the urge to gulp the bottled water you have. Use buckets, clean food containers, or anything else that will hold water to collect rain.

### 4. Fish for Food.
Make a simple fishing line out of string or a shoelace. Bend anything small and metal—a soda can tab, jewelry, a safety pin—into a hook, tie it to the end of your line, and dangle it into the water, using bits of food for bait. You can also scoop up seaweed to eat.

### 5. Shield the Sun.

This is not the time to work on your tan. The sun can be harsh on open water, and that can lead to severe sunburn, dehydration, even sun poisoning. Put on sunscreen, wear a hat and sunglasses, and cover exposed skin with towels.

### 6. Signaling Smarts.

If you see a ship in the distance, or a low-flying plane or helicopter, it's time to make a scene! Use your flare gun or signaling device. If you don't have those things, use a mirror to reflect light or wave something colorful as if your life depended on it, because it very well might.

### 7. The Bird Is the Word.

If you're stranded on the ocean, look for seabirds. Many head back to land at dusk. If it's getting late and you see a bird winging over-head, paddle after it. It just might lead you to land.

### 8. Look for Land.

Even a deserted island is better than floating on open water. Once you land, you can set up camp and wait for help. Use big rocks to spell out an SOS, or lay something brightly colored on the beach to attract attention.

# Lost in the Woods

Maybe you took a detour or got separated from your group. You might even have slipped and hurt yourself. Here's how to make sure you don't end up living like a hermit in the wilderness.

### I. Plan Ahead.
ALWAYS tell someone where you're going and what time you'll be back. Make sure your phone is fully charged. Even if your service isn't great, you might be able to ping your location. It's also a good idea to pack water, snacks, and a paper map—or at least download one to your device. GPS doesn't always work in the wilderness! A flashlight and matches in a watertight container are also good to have. And dress appropriately—wear sturdy shoes or hiking boots and light layers, and bring a jacket.

### 2. Stay Put.
You've probably worn yourself out backtracking and trying new paths. Pick a spot and stay there. Choose a flat, dry spot that can be seen from the air or that is close to water.

### 3. Make a Scene.
You want your new home to be easy to see. Tie extra clothes or your backpack to the trees at eye level to make yourself more visible.

### 4. Make Some Noise!
If you hear rescuers—or anyone, for that matter—it's no time to be shy! Scream for help, call out, "I'm here!" or just holler.

### 5. Make Shelter.
If it's getting dark, it's time to settle in for the night. If you can find a big branch, prop it against a tree and place other branches

around it to make a rough shelter. Fill in the gaps with mud and leaves. Yeah, it's messy and not exactly home, sweet home, but it may protect you from the cold.

### 6. What's for Dinner?

Hopefully, you packed some portable snacks. It's fine to eat a few, but don't scarf them all down—you don't know how long you'll be stranded. If you're REALLY sure about what's poisonous and what isn't, you might be able to find edible berries or plants to eat. As for water, streams can contain bacteria, so you may not want to drink from them unless you brought water-purifying tablets or you get really desperate. Instead, ration the water you brought with you, collect rainwater, or even suck dew from plants.

### Ouch!

What if you're hurt? Here are a few quick tips to get you through:

- If you're bleeding, use an item of clothing to put pressure on the wound until the bleeding stops.
- Wrap something around the wound to keep the injury clean and dry. You can tear up your shirt to make bandages.
- Use your shirt or jacket to make a sling for an injured arm.
- Need to make a splint? Tie a branch to the injured arm or leg using strips of torn-up clothing or supple branches or grass.

# Lost in the Desert

The desert is an amazing place, but it can also be very dangerous. Here's what to do to keep this excursion into this extreme habitat from turning into a disaster.

## I. Check In Before You Head Out.
Always tell someone where you're going and what time you expect to be back.

## 2. Pack a Survival Kit.
Even a short trip into the desert can turn bad, but packing the right things will help you survive. Be sure to bring:

- Water and plenty of it. Always carry more than you think you'll need. Bring at least two liters per person on a day hike, more if you're planning to stay longer.
- Personal locator beacon. These little devices send a satellite signal that can help rescuers pinpoint exactly where you are, even when you don't have phone service.
- Extra food. Trail mix, protein or granola bars, and fruit are not only great snacks, they can help you keep your energy up.
- Sunscreen. The desert sun is brutal! And you may not find much natural shade. Bring sunglasses and a hat too.
- Paper map and compass.
- A first aid kit.
- A whistle to signal rescuers.
- A mirror, also great for signaling.
- Matches.
- Did we mention water?

### 3. Stay Calm.
Panicking will not help. Stay calm, try to figure where you are, and make a plan.

### 4. Don't Drink the Cactus Juice.
Some people believe that a cactus is filled with water, so they will cut one open. This is a terrible idea! Cactus juice can make you very sick. And pulling cactus spines out of your fingers won't help either.

### 5. Made in the Shade.
During the hottest hours of the day (usually about 10 a.m. to 3 p.m.), try to find shade, such as on the side of a rock or under a bush or tree, and stay put.

### 6. Keep Your Clothes On.
It's hot, and your first inclination might be to strip down. But this exposes more of your skin, which can lead to a bad sunburn, heat exhaustion, and worse.

### 7. Watch Out for Wildlife.
Deserts are home to poisonous creatures, including scorpions, rattlesnakes, and Gila monsters. Be careful around rocks, as there may be a dangerous critter hiding underneath, and always watch where you step.

### 8. Nighttime Is the Right Time.
Deserts can be freezing cold at night. Build a fire to stay warm and signal rescuers. Put on all your layers of clothes. Nighttime is also a good time for walking in search of fuel for the fire or a water source.

### 9. Beware of Floods.
Floods in the desert? Yes, really, flash floods can happen quickly. Stay out of low valleys, canyons, or dry riverbeds. Staying on higher ground will keep you safer.

# Lost in a Cave

Have you heard the story of the soccer team that spent more than two weeks trapped in a flooded cave? That was an extreme situation, but a cave can be a scary place to be trapped. Here are some tips to survive:

- Always go exploring with others. Experts recommend having at least four people in your group. Kids should always be with an adult.
- Caves flood easily, so check the weather before you go, and postpone your trip if rain is in the forecast.
- Bring supplies. Water, food, flashlights and extra batteries, a poncho or raincoat, matches in a waterproof container, a whistle, and a first aid kit are must-haves.
- Wear sturdy shoes and layers of clothing. Protect your hands with gloves and bring knee and elbow pads in case you have to crawl through tight places.
- Walk carefully and avoid jumping or running. Pay attention to your surroundings and note landmarks that can guide you.
- If you get lost, look for clues that might lead you to the surface, such as light and warm air. Stay on paths that travel upward. Stay calm and focused.
- Make a trail out of rocks or scraps of paper—anything that will help you backtrack if you get even more lost.
- NEVER drink cave water.
- If you have no idea which direction to go, stay put. Find a flat place, preferably above the cave floor, and set up camp until help arrives.

# Lost in a City

Big cities can be scary and confusing places for a stranger! However, there are lots of things you can do to find your way back to a familiar place.

- Don't get scared. Remember, you're in a big city, not outer space. There are plenty of people around who can help you.
- Got a phone? Use a maps app to pinpoint where you are and locate nearby landmarks. If possible, look for street signs or familiar signs. If you know someone in the city, call them and ask them to meet you.
- If you're in a city where you don't speak the local language well, write down the name of your hotel or destination in that language. That way you can show the paper and ask for help even if you can't ask clearly.
- Memorize basic phrases in the local language, such as "Hello," "Can you help?", "Excuse me," and "Please."
- Don't be afraid to ask for help. Most people are kind and happy to assist.
- If you don't feel safe, look for a public building with lots of people. Store clerks or security guards are good people to ask for help. So are workers in transit centers, like bus or train stations, or hotels.
- Look for a police officer. Traffic cops know their way around!
- Be observant. Look for landmarks, street signs, or stores. You can use these clues to lead you back to where you started.

# WHEN
# NATURE
# ATTACKS

# Staying Safe in a Hurricane

High winds. Torrential rain. Ferocious flooding. Hurricanes have it all. The good news is that you'll have plenty of warning if a hurricane is headed your way. Here's how to prepare:

### I. Be Informed.
Listen to the news and sign up for location-specific weather alerts. Know where the storm is heading and if and when it's going to strike near you.

### 2. Prepare!
Discuss an emergency plan with your family so you know where to go and how to contact each other in case you get separated.

### 3. Get Home Ready.
You can protect your home from damage by boarding up windows or putting up storm shutters. It's also important to bring in or tie down any outdoor objects that could turn into airborne projectiles. That includes garbage cans, outdoor furniture, grills, and yard decorations.

### 4. Should I Stay, or Should I Go?
If your local government imposes a mandatory evacuation, don't stay at home. Get out, following local evacuation routes. Leave as early as possible and bring food, water, and blankets because you'll probably be in for a long ride.

## 5. Staying Safe at Home.

If you don't have to evacuate, find an interior room without windows to shelter in. Hurricanes tend to last for many hours, so you'll probably end up sleeping there. The power will probably go out, so have flashlights, phone chargers, extra batteries, and a battery-powered radio handy.

## 6. No Power? No Problem!

Hurricanes often knock out power, sometimes for days. Fill up your bathtub so you have water for flushing toilets. Keep your refrigerator and freezer door closed. Food will stay colder longer if you do.

## 7. Stay Inside!

Hurricanes are tricky because they move in a circular motion, which creates a calm area called the eye in the middle of the storm. The sun might even come out! But don't be fooled—there's more dangerous weather on the way.

## 8. Explore with Care.

After the storm is over, you'll probably want to go outside and explore, and check on your neighbors. Be careful! There may be downed trees or branches. There are probably downed wires too. Stay away from wires, flooded areas, and any metal objects.

# Tornado Rules

There's no denying that a tornado is one of the scariest and most powerful storms on Earth. If a tornado is headed your way, here's what to do:

### I. Know Your Watches and Warnings.
A tornado watch means that weather conditions could produce a tornado. A warning means a tornado has been spotted and could be headed your way.

### 2. Go Deep.
If you have a basement, cellar, or storm shelter, get there now! If not, go to a room without windows on the lowest floor. Having your whole family crammed into a closet may be uncomfortable, but it could save your lives.

### 3. Furniture Can Be Your Friend.
Hiding under a sturdy desk or table can be a lifesaver. But stay away from heavy furniture that might fall on you, such as a refrigerator or a bookcase. Cover yourself with couch cushions, a mattress, blankets, or anything else that will protect you.

### 4. Outdoor Safety.
If you're outside when a tornado comes along, try to find shelter. If all else fails, find a ditch or low area away from trees and lie down flat, with your hands over your head.

### 5. Proceed with Caution.
When you go outside after the storm, watch out for debris, downed trees and wires, and other dangers.

# Flood Safety

The water is rising! Here's how to stay safe (but maybe not dry!) in a flood.

### I. Be Prepared.
Have an emergency kit packed. It's a good idea to keep a kit in the car as well.

### 2. Listen and Obey.
If you receive a flood warning or an evacuation order, GO! You need to get away before flood waters arrive.

### 3. Get High.
Stay away from basements and low-lying areas. Move to an upper floor or, if you're outside, head for higher ground.

### 4. Watch for Debris.
Flood waters are very powerful, and they carry away everything in their path: branches, furniture, even pieces of buildings. Be alert for live power lines.

### 5. No Swimming.
Don't try to walk or drive through water. Just six inches of water can sweep a person off their feet, and two feet of moving water can wash away a car. And that water is probably contaminated with sewage or chemicals that could make you sick.

### 6. Dress for Success.
After a flood, protect your body by wearing heavy shoes, long pants, and gloves.

# Earthquake Alert

Did you feel the earth move under your feet? Here's what to do if the world starts to shake, rattle, and roll.

### 1. Hide Out and Hold On.
You're more likely to be hurt by falling debris than by the earth shifting. So get underneath a table or desk, or stand in a doorway.

### 2. Move Away.
Move away from anything that might fall. Bookcases, TVs, and chandeliers are not your friends. In fact, outside in an open field could be your safest bet.

### 3. Take the Stairs.
NEVER use an elevator during or after a quake. The power is likely to go out and you'll be stranded.

### 4. Watch Out for Waves.
Earthquakes often trigger huge waves called tsunamis. If you're in a coastal area, stay away from the beach. In fact, head for the highest ground you can find.

### 5. Keep Tapping.
If you're trapped under debris, tap on metal or a hard part of the structure to let rescuers know where you are. Don't waste your energy or voice yelling for help unless you hear rescuers nearby.

> ⚠️ **SAFETY TIP: Your Earthquake Mantra**
> There are four words to remember during an earthquake: Drop, Cover, and Hold On. So **Drop** to your hands and knees so you don't fall. **Cover** your body, especially your head and neck. And **Hold On** to whatever you're sheltering under.

# Winter Storm Watch

Here's how to stay safe so you can have an epic snowball fight after the storm passes.

### 1. Be a Weather Watcher.
Weather reports often forecast big winter storms several days ahead of time. If a major ice or snowstorm is forecast, make plans to stay home.

### 2. Snuggle Up.
Remember that emergency kit? Make sure yours is ready. A blizzard can block roads and knock out power, so you might be stuck inside for awhile. Have plenty of blankets and sleeping bags to ward off the cold. Never use the kitchen oven or a backyard grill inside to keep warm—it's not safe.

### 3. Layer Up.
If you're caught away from home, it's important to stay warm. Dress in layers, and don't forget warm boots, gloves or mittens, a scarf, and a hat.

### 4. Shelter from the Storm.
If you're stranded outside, seek shelter. If there's no place to wait out the storm, try to build a shelter by tunneling into the snow. Thirsty? Always melt snow before drinking it.

### 5. Stock Your Car.
Make sure the family car has a shovel, an ice scraper/snow brush, some sand or kitty litter (great for providing traction if you're stuck), blankets, a flashlight with extra batteries, road flares, and some food and water. Stay in your car if you get stuck. You can run the motor for 10 minutes every hour to warm up, but be sure to clear snow away from the exhaust pipe first.

# Raging Wildfires

Wildfires can spread quicker than you think. Luckily, there are ways to protect yourself.

- Remove any brush around your house, trim back trees, and make sure firewood is stored at least 30 feet away from buildings. Remove leaves and twigs from under decks and around foundations.
- Prepare an evacuation kit, with prescription medications, important paperwork and photos, phone chargers, food, water, and pet supplies.
- Know your evacuation route *before* an emergency occurs.
- If your area receives an evacuation order, leave right away! The roads will be packed, and you don't want to be in a traffic jam when flames arrive.
- Close windows and vents to keep out smoke. Cover your mouth and nose with clothing or wet towels.
- If you're in a car and get trapped by a raging fire, do not get out of the car. Roll up the windows, lie on the floor, and cover yourself with a blanket until the fire passes.
- If you're trapped outside, lie down on the ground away from vegetation. Cover your body and protect your face.
- Call 911 if you are trapped.

# Eruption Safety

Odds are there are no volcanoes in your neighborhood. But there are more than a few volcanoes in the United States, and you never know when one might erupt!

- Listen to scientists. Volcanoes give off lots of clues before they erupt, and experts will be monitoring the situation.
- Evacuate immediately if you are told to do so. Plan a route away from the volcano before disaster strikes.
- Never drive around barricades or try to get close to an erupting volcano. This is not the time to post videos!
- If you're indoors, stay there. Close all windows, doors, and vents. Turn off air conditioners. Bring pets inside.
- Shelter on an upper floor, if possible, to avoid poisonous fumes.
- If you're outside, roll into a ball and protect your head and face. Cover yourself with a jacket or blanket if you can.
- Volcanoes are more than just lava. Watch out for floods, falling rocks, avalanches, and mudflows.
- Ash fall is a big problem during an eruption. Wear a mask or cover your nose and mouth. Wear goggles to protect your eyes.
- If ash fall is heavy, don't stand under a deck or porch. These structures can collapse from the weight of the ash.
- Avoid driving in heavy ash fall, as your car engine can stall.
- Seek medical treatment ASAP if you are burned or you have trouble breathing.

# Watch Out for Rip Tides!

It's a beautiful day at the beach, and you dive into the water. Everything is going great, until suddenly the current is pulling you far from shore. You're caught in a rip tide!

## Rip Tide Escape Route

- Stay calm. Panicking will only tire you out and make things worse.
- Signal for help. Wave or call out to people on shore for help.
- Don't try to head to shore. The rip tide is stronger than you are, and you'll just tire yourself out.
- Swim parallel to the shoreline. If you get tired, float or tread water.
- Look for a spot where waves are breaking onto the beach. That's a sign that you've escaped the rip tide. Now you can swim or float to shore.

# Avalanche!

You're out on the slopes when you see something strange. The mountain is moving! Don't want to be buried in tons of snow? Take these avalanche precautions.

- Be aware. Make sure there are no avalanche warnings in your area.
- Travel with a group and with supplies, such as a beacon, an airbag, and a helmet.
- Watch for danger signs. Cracks in the snow or booming noises are bad news.
- If you see an avalanche, get off your skis or snowboard.
- Move in a diagonal direction away from the avalanche, or move toward the edges, where the snow is not as deep.
- If the snow overtakes you, pretend you're in a river of water and move your arms like you're swimming to try to stay on top of the snow.
- Close your mouth. You don't want a mouthful of snow!
- Curve your arms in front of your head and chest to make space. If you're buried, this can create an air pocket that will help you survive.
- Stick up an arm or a ski pole (if you still have them nearby).
- Don't waste air and energy yelling. Wait until you hear voices or shovels digging. Then it's time to yell!

# When Lightning Strikes

You're having fun outside when the sky gets dark and thunder rumbles. Are you about to become a human lightning rod? Not if you take these safety steps!

- If you're swimming or boating, get out of or off of the water as fast as possible.
- Move away from trees or other tall objects. Lightning loves to strike tall things.
- Stay away from anything metal, such as benches or fences.
- Try to shelter in a building or a car.
- If you're with friends, spread out so you don't become part of a chain reaction.
- If there's nowhere to hide, move to the lowest point you can find. Crouch down on the ground with your hands over your head.
- If you're inside, you can take some steps to stay safe—indoor lightning strikes are very rare but not impossible. Don't go near water or use any electronics that are plugged in—lightning can travel through the wires!
- Stay off of porches and away from windows and doors.
- Do not leave shelter until at least 30 minutes after thunder stops.

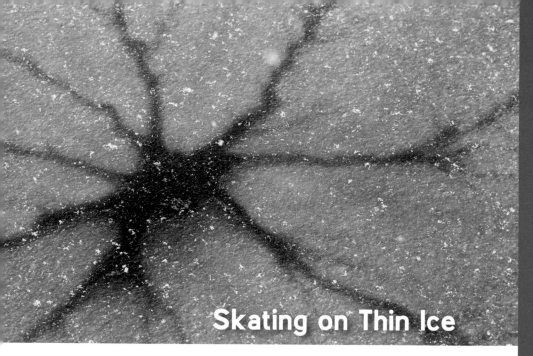

# Skating on Thin Ice

Snap, crackle, pop! No, it's not your favorite breakfast cereal talking. It's the ice under your feet, and you're about to become a human popsicle! Follow these tips for safety on the ice.

- Nothing is better than staying out of danger in the first place. Obey all thin ice warnings and never ignore a red flag on the ice. You can play hockey another day.
- Never go out on ice that is less than four inches thick. And remember that just because one spot has thick ice, other areas may not.
- Never go on the ice alone.
- If you hear ice cracking under your feet, lie flat and spread out your arms and legs.
- Roll away from the crack.
- If you fall through the surface, don't panic! Put your hands and then your arms on the edge of the ice. Slowly inch your way forward while kicking your feet. Once you're on the ice, roll away from the hole.
- If you spot a person that has fallen through the ice, call 911 immediately. Don't get close to the hole, or you're likely to fall in as well. Instead, use a rope, a board, a tree limb, even a jacket to pull the person to safety.
- Go home immediately for dry clothes and a hot beverage.

## Help! It's Quicksand!

It seems like quicksand is a big problem in old movies and TV shows but in the real world, quicksand is pretty rare. Still, accidents happen, so keep these tips in mind.

- Quicksand is found in wet areas, so be careful walking along rivers, streams, ponds, or swampy places.
- Quicksand is denser than the human body. So although you can get stuck, you're not going to sink to the bottom.
- Don't panic or thrash around. Slow and steady movements are the answer.
- Lean back to spread out your weight.
- Lighten up! Toss aside backpacks, shoes, canteens, anything that will weigh you down.
- Keep your arms up.
- Try to move backward, away from the squishiness.
- Reach for something to pull you out—a tree branch, a vine, your best friend's hand.

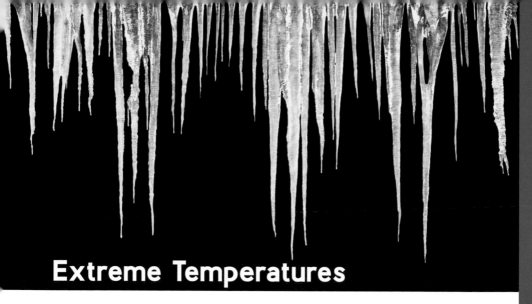

# Extreme Temperatures

If you get too hot for too long or too cold for too long, you—or your limbs—might not make it. Here's what to do when the thermometer threatens.

### Preventing Frostbite
Wear thin layers and change your clothes when they get wet. Try to take breaks indoors every 15-20 minutes when it's very cold. If the temperature or windchill is below –15° F (–26° C), just stay inside.

### Signs of Frostbite

- Skin that is paler than normal, cold, and hard
- Pain, tingling, burning, numbness, or aching
- Swelling or blisters in the first 24 hours
- Later signs include dark purple or black skin and no feeling or pain in that part of the body

### Treating Frostbite
It is always best to get treated by a medical professional. But if you can't, start rewarming the skin right away, with wet heat, like warm, damp washcloths, or a basin of warm (not hot!) water.

> ⚠ **SAFETY TIP: The Heat Is On**
> Heat stroke or heat exhaustion is no joke. If you have any of the warning signs, like heavy sweating, pale skin, headache, nausea, and dizziness, take action. Get to a cooler place, sip water, and cool yourself with wet cloths or a lukewarm bath. If you faint or lose consciousness, get medical help immediately.

# FAMILY TROUBLES

# Surviving Embarrassing Parents

Oh no! Is your dad really going to wear that old holey sweater out in public ... again? Is your mom actually dancing to the lame music in the grocery store? It's not like they're embarrassing you on purpose (at least, not most of the time!). So how can you deal with these cringey people you live with? Here's a few ideas.

## I. Look Beyond the Moment.
Your parents might have very good reasons for the embarrassing things they say and do. For example, when your mom repeats the story of how you smeared chocolate pudding all over your face when you were a baby, she's not trying to embarrass you. She's just remembering a sweet, funny moment and feeling sentimental for your baby years.

## 2. Let Them Have Fun.
You might cringe when your dad sings his favorite old song at the top of his lungs. But look at it this way—Dad loves that song and singing it makes him happy. The same is true when your mom wears a ratty T-shirt that makes her remember a fun trip with an old friend. Sometimes you just have to grin and bear it, and let your parents have their happy moments.

## 3. Put the Shoe on the Other Foot.
Sure, your parents are embarrassing you now, but what about all the times you embarrassed them? Did you throw a tantrum in a restaurant when you were a toddler? Did you say something rude about a relative to their face? We've all had some moments that made our parents want to sink through the floor.

## 4. Solutions, Not Threats.
When you speak to your parents, work together to find a solution. Saying, "I would appreciate it if you only called me 'Cuddlebug' at

home and not at school" is better than screaming, "Don't ever talk to me in public again!"

### 5. Speak Up.
Make a list of three or four things your parents do that really, really bother you. Then talk to your parents. Make it clear that you love them, and ask them nicely if they could be more aware of just a few things and stop doing them. You could even come up with a signal together that tells them, "You're doing it again! Please stop."

### 6. Keep It Cool.
You might want to make a scene when your parents embarrass you for the millionth time, but does that really help? Or does it just draw more attention to the situation and truly make you look ridiculous? Ignore and move on. You can always talk to your parents later, in private.

### 7. Remember, We All Have Parents.
Believe it or not, you aren't the first or the only person to want to disappear after your parents say or do something ridiculous. Your friends have parents too, and it's guaranteed that they have gone off the rails a few times. Feeling confident that your friends will understand because they've been through the same thing can make you feel a lot better.

### 8. Live With It.
It's sad but true: Changing your behavior is hard. And maybe your parents don't see what the big deal is, or just brush you off when you try to explain how you feel. If this happens, try not to dwell on it too much. Just remember, one day you could be a parent, and your kids will complain about you!

# Family Fight Club

One sibling makes a mean joke, the other steals your favorite shirt AGAIN, and the next thing you know, everyone needs a time out— including your parents! If things get out of control at home, here are some ways to make peace.

## Parent Problems

### 1. Break Time.
It's hard to think clearly in the heat of the moment. Instead of continuing the fight, take a break. Agree to discuss the issue later, once you've calmed down. You might even make an appointment: "Let's talk about this after dinner. Meet in the kitchen at 8:00."

### 2. Make a Plan.
Instead of sulking, use that cooling-off period to think about what you hope to achieve. For example, if you want to sleep over at your friend's house, list the reasons why your parents should say yes. Think of reasons they've said no and come up with a response to each that might change their minds.

### 3. Communicate Clearly.
Instead of shouting, speak calmly and clearly to get your point across so your parents can really hear you.

### 4. Be an Active Listener.
You want your parents to listen to your point of view, right? But respect goes both ways, so listen to what they have to say as well. That means no interrupting, and not just focusing on what you're going to say back to them.

### 5. Watch Your Language!

Body language, that is. Rolling your eyes or crossing your arms across your chest will not win you any points.

### 6. Use Good Words, Not Bad Words.

Phrases like "I understand that . . ." and "I hear you saying . . ." can show how you're interpreting their point of view. For example, "I understand that what I'm asking for costs more money than you want to spend," or "I'm hearing that you are afraid to let me be out alone after dark." Bad words to use include "always" and "never," as in: "You never let me have any fun" or "You're always telling me what to do."

### 7. Try to Compromise.

Look for options that both of you can live with. Your parents might let you go to that party if you promise to text them a few times during the night. (Side note: Be sure to keep the promises you make! That builds trust and will help you win more arguments in the future.)

## Sibling Smackdown

- **Keep Cool.** There are many good reasons conflict happens, but there are also many good reasons NOT to fight. Try to "keep calm and carry on," instead of turning into Godzilla every time your sibs annoy you.
- **Discuss, Don't Fuss.** Instead of screaming, make a pact to discuss the issue calmly. Dialing down the temperature can get better results than name-calling, making accusations, or getting physical.
- **Don't Get Physical.** Hitting, punching, kicking, and any kind of violence is never okay. It won't get you want you want, and it might get you or someone else hurt.
- **Walk Away.** If things get physical, it's okay to walk away. Don't try to one-up the other person or refuse to back down. It's okay to take the space you need to calm down.
- **Ask for Help.** No one likes a tattletale, but if every disagreement with your siblings turns into a screaming match or worse, it's time to get a neutral referee involved. An older sibling might do the trick, or meet as a family and try to work out a solution that pleases everyone.

# Big Trouble at Home

All families have problems. Unfortunately, some families have BIG problems like addiction, mental illness, and domestic violence—problems that are way too big to handle alone.

- Remember that addiction, mental illness, and abuse are powerful forces that can make people act in ways they never would otherwise. It is important to remember that these things are not your fault. You are not the cause of other people's problems.
- Speak to an adult you trust. Talk to a counselor at school or a favorite teacher or coach. People with these jobs are trained to take action and will know how to get help.
- If the first adult you talk to doesn't help, talk to someone else. Don't give up!
- Look for a safe place to turn. Can you stay at a friend's house or with a grandparent? If you feel unsafe, you need to get out of the situation. Call 911 or your local police if you need immediate help.
- Call or text a hotline. Most communities have hotlines to get help for addiction, abuse, mental illness, and more. These can guide you on what steps to take next.

> ⚠ **SAFETY TIP: When Silence Isn't Golden**
> It's normal to want to hide bad news. You might be embarrassed to admit your family isn't perfect, or you might be worried about what others will think. Or you might be scared that speaking up will make things worse or get a family member in trouble. But the truth is, problems don't go away by themselves. So don't be afraid to talk it over with someone you trust.

## Staying Home Alone

Staying home alone means you're growing up and that your parents trust you. But being "king of the castle" can sometimes be scary too. Here are some tips to make it a good time.

- Follow all your parents' rules, even if you think they're dumb.
- Save contact information on your phone for parents, neighbors, other relatives, and the police and fire department.
- Lock the doors. If your house has a security system, know how to turn it on and off.
- Don't answer the door or let anyone in the house who you don't know.
- Don't give out personal information over the phone or tell anyone your parents aren't home. Better yet, just let calls go to voice mail.
- Go over the rules with your parents. Are you allowed to have a friend over? Can you order takeout? Find out before you act.
- Don't cook or use the stove or oven without permission.
- Discuss what to do if an emergency happens.
- Don't post on social media that you're home alone.
- Don't leave the house unless you've cleared it with your parents first.
- Did you hear a scary noise outside? Stay inside and call your parents or a neighbor to investigate.
- Don't throw a huge party and expect to get away with it. This is real life, not the movies.

# Help! My Parents Are Splitting Up!

You probably feel like someone took your home and threw it up in the air, letting the pieces scatter all over the place. But parents deciding to separate doesn't have to be the end of the world.

### 1. No Blame Game.
Repeat after us: The divorce is not your fault. Your parents are adults with problems that have nothing to do with you.

### 2. Feel the Love.
Remember that your parents might not love each other the same way anymore, but they still love you. That shouldn't change, even though many other things are going to be different.

### 3. Roll With the Changes.
Expect a lot of things to be different, even if you don't know exactly how things will change right away. You might split your time between your parents instead of living with both of them. Or you might not see one parent very often anymore. You might have to move to a new neighborhood. Change is hard, no lie, but tell yourself you are strong, and you can get through this.

### 4. Choose Carefully.
It's easy to make bad choices when you're upset or angry. But bad decisions will only make things worse. Instead of running wild, talk to friends who will support you, take part in an activity that makes you happy, or write your feelings in a journal.

### 5. Read (or Watch) All About It.

There are many, many books, movies, and TV shows about divorced families. Ask your favorite librarian for recommendations on the topic and get some ideas of how other kids have coped.

### 6. Speak Up!

It's normal to feel scared, sad, even angry at what life has thrown at you. It might help to talk to someone about your feelings. Let your parents know how you feel and what you need from them. Don't want to confide in a family member? Talk to a counselor, nurse, or teacher at school, or another adult you trust. They should be able to guide you to resources—or just provide a listening ear.

### 7. Empathy Rules.

As hard as things are for you, try to understand that others may be hurting too, your parents and siblings included. The more you can try to understand how others around you are feeling and that no one is perfectly happy all the time—especially when things are difficult!—the less alone you're bound to feel.

# Surviving "Steps"

As if getting divorced wasn't enough change, now there is some stranger is living in your house and even telling you what to do. Try these tips instead of losing your temper.

- Expect change. You might have to share your bedroom with a new sibling, or accept changes in family routines.
- Understand that it's normal to feel sad, angry, or upset. Let your parents know how you feel.
- Look for activities or events you can enjoy as a family.
- Look for common interests. Maybe your stepsister enjoys basketball as much as you do, or your stepbrother has an awesome graphic novel collection.
- Follow family rules but DO speak up if you feel they are unfair or if you're getting different versions from different adults.
- Don't play family members against each other.
- Be fair. Don't disregard advice just because a stepparent said it. Ask yourself if you would react the same way if your "real" mom or dad said the same thing.
- Don't expect a happy family right away. Your family is not the "Brady Bunch" from the 1970s! While it's great if you can get along, there are going to be bumps along the way.

- R-E-S-P-E-C-T. You may not agree with your new family members. You may not even like them all that much. But you should always respect them and insist that they respect you in return.

## It's Not Just "Steps"!

Divorce and remarriage are not the only ways families can change. You might have a grandparent or another adult relative move in with you, or a new baby or a foster child, or a family friend. When your family shape starts to change, talk to your parents about how the changes will affect all of you. Will you have to give up your room? Keep different schedules that include quiet hours? Give up an activity? Be asked to help more around the house?

Knowing what to expect can make things easier on everyone. And, just like with blended families, showing respect, being willing to adapt, and making an effort to get along will help make the situation a happy one.

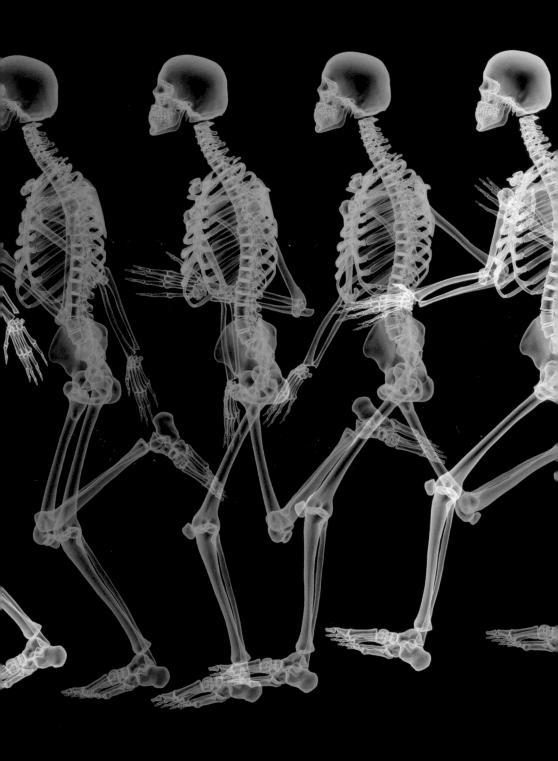

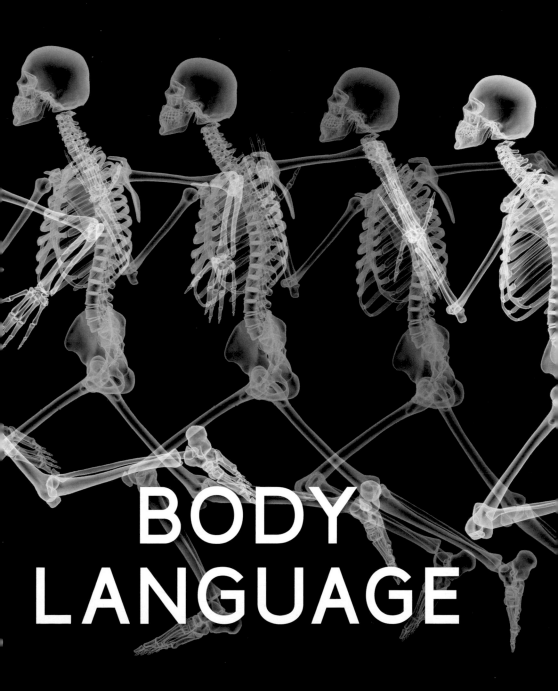

BODY
LANGUAGE

# Hey, Four Eyes!

Wearing glasses is not as bad or inconvenient as you think. Try these strategies to feel good and be able to see the world clearly.

- Find a style that works for you. Glasses come in all sorts of colors, shapes, and styles. There's bound to be a pair that makes you look awesome!
- Think of glasses as a new accessory, like a cool backpack or pair of sneakers.
- Lots of kids wear glasses. This may be new for you, but it's not like you're showing up at school with an extra head.

- Lots of celebrities wear glasses too—and some just wear them for the fashion! Google photos of popular singers, athletes, or actors with glasses.
- Make a list of the good things about wearing glasses. Wearing glasses means you won't have to squint or miss out on details. You won't have to sit right in front of the white board. And hopefully you'll stop getting headaches from staring at your screen.
- Talk to your parents and your eye doctor about your worries. They'll probably have some suggestions to make you feel more comfortable.
- You might not have to wear glasses forever. Contacts and even, eventually, vision surgery are options for many people. For now, look at the world with pride in your eyes!

## A Hairy Situation

Maybe someone got a little carried away with the clippers and now you're stuck with a shaved head. Or your new style makes you look like you had a close encounter with a lightning bolt. Since you can't wear a bag over your head for the next month, try these tips.

- Change it up. Sometimes a bad haircut can be salvaged by washing out all the gunk the hair salon put in, or—just the opposite—adding mousse or gel to shape your hair into a better look.
- Try some tools. Experiment with a curling iron or a flat iron to change your hair's shape or texture.
- See if someone can fix your hair. If the stylist knows you're unhappy, they might fix your hair for free. Or you can try going to a different stylist. You might even get a parent or a friend to work on your hair (note: this can be risky!).
- Add accessories. Clip it back or pull your hair up into a bun. Try adding clip-on extensions in fun colors.
- Just want to cover up? Try wearing a bandana, a headband, a scarf, or your favorite hat. Who knows, you might start a new trend!
- Keep telling yourself that it's only hair, and it will grow out. No bad haircut lasts forever!

# Pimple Problems

When you were a little kid, you probably didn't worry about your skin. Your face looked the same, other than the occasional scrape or cut or sunburn. But what if when you look in the mirror, all you can see are pimples? The good news is, there are ways to cope.

- Don't pick at your skin or try to pop pimples. This will only make your skin more irritated and can even leave scars.
- Wash your face regularly. Be gentle—no ferocious scrubbing!
- See a dermatologist —a skin doctor. They can advise you on a healthy routine and help you decide if you need prescription medicine to help your skin calm down.
- Some acne treatments work by drying up oil, but this can make your skin extremely dry. Be sure to use moisturizers to combat the dryness. Your doctor will have some suggestions.
- Be patient. It can take time for treatments to start working.
- Understand that you're not the only person going through this. Bad skin happens to everyone.
- Remember that you are more than just your face. Of course, it's hard to feel confident when you don't look your best, but your skin is just one part of your awesome self!

# You Stink!

What's that awful smell? Oh no, it's you! As we enter our tweens and teens, our bodies go a little haywire. New hormones show up, and they cause all kinds of physical changes. Unfortunately, one of those is increased body odor. Here are some tips to stop your friends from keeping their distance.

- Keep it clean. Shower every day or after physical activity. Use soap and clean places that get stinky more easily, such as pits, feet, and private parts. Washing with soap and water doesn't just remove dirt, it gets rid of yucky bacteria too.
- Wear deodorant or anti-perspirant. What's the difference? Deodorants help stop odor, while anti-perspirants help stop sweat. Try different brands until you find one you like. There are natural options too.
- Don't wear the same shirt for a week. Seriously, clean clothes smell better than dirty ones. And do you really want to wear smelly, grimy clothes?
- Feet are a source of super-stink. Wear clean socks and be sure to wash between your toes.
- Poor hygiene can cause bad breath. Be sure to brush and floss regularly.
- If all else fails, ask your parents to take you to the doctor. Sometimes there is a medical reason for a funky smell.
- Don't be embarrassed to talk about hygiene with your doctor. They'll be the first to tell you that they have heard—and smelled!—a lot worse.

# Drinking, Drugs, and Other Dangers

How many times have you heard that drinking, taking unprescribed drugs, smoking, or vaping are bad for you? Probably so many times that you've tuned it out. We could write a whole book on the dangers of drugs, but for now, keep these facts in mind.

### I. They're Poisons!
Vapes, cigarettes, alcohol, and drugs put harmful chemicals in your body. Those chemicals *might* make you feel good, but they can *definitely* do terrible things to your health.

### 2. They Lead to Bad Decisions.
Alcohol and drugs can affect a person's judgment, and that can lead to people doing terrible things. Driving drunk or high is the best example of this, but there are many other ways to get hurt—or killed.

### 3. They Mess With Your Brain.
Your brain and lungs are still developing—do you really want to damage them? The future might seem far away, but we're pretty sure you'll want to breathe and think clearly all your life.

### 4. They Make You Feel Bad.
The truth is that any pleasure is short-term, and substance abuse can feed anxiety, depression, and worse.

### 5. Everyone Is NOT Doing It.
It might seem like a lot of people you know are experimenting with drugs or alcohol, but that's just perception. Plenty of kids do NOT partake.

# Hospital Horrors?

Being in the hospital is not on anybody's wish list. Along with not feeling well, you're stuck in a strange, unfriendly place. Keep these tips in mind if you're facing a hospital stay.

- **Connect with family.** A parent or caregiver might be able to stay in the hospital with you. Otherwise, stay close through video calls, texts, and chats.
- **Ask questions.** Doctors, therapists, and nurses are there to help you get better, and they should be happy to help you understand what's going on.
- **Bring a bit of home.** If you can, pack a comfort object, like a favorite teddy bear or blanket.
- **Stay in touch.** Have friends and family visit or call often, and don't be shy about requesting items from the outside.
- **Stay active.** If you can get up, take walks around the floor. Many hospitals have playrooms or lounges and outdoor areas.
- **Express yourself.** Keep a journal, draw a picture, or record a video to vent your feelings.
- **Feel it out.** Understand that it's okay to feel scared, anxious, and angry. No one is at their best when they don't feel well.

⚠ **SAFETY TIP: Hospital Visits**

Visiting someone in the hospital can be scary. There are weird machines, odd noises, and strange smells. The patient you're visiting might not look the way you are used to and they might not feel up to talking. But try to be brave and hang out for a bit. It's fine if you can't stay long, or if you feel scared. Just remember, you're there to help the other person, and they'll be glad you cared enough to visit.

# Open Wide and Say AAAHHH!

We're guessing the dentist is not your favorite place. But taking care of your teeth is super important, so here are some ways to get through a dentist visit.

- Talk to a parent about what to expect at the dentist.
- Ask questions about what the dentist is going to do. Routine dental procedures, such as cleanings, can be uncomfortable, but they usually don't hurt.
- Speak up! It's okay to admit you're scared about what the dentist is doing.
- Stay calm. Breathe deeply. Try to think of something else while the dentist is working. Run through what you have planned for your upcoming weekend or holiday celebration in order, or make a to-do list for the rest of your day.

- If you need a cavity filled or another procedure, ask (or have your parent ask) what kind of pain relief you should expect to have.
- If the dentist has to give you a shot in your mouth, try not to freak out. Close your eyes and picture yourself in your happy place. The shot will only take a second, and it shouldn't hurt that much.
- Arrange a signal, such as raising your hand, that shows you need the dentist to stop for a moment.
- Bring a favorite toy or stuffed animal to hold.
- Some dentists show movies or play music. If yours doesn't, ask if it's okay to listen to something using earbuds.

# Brace Face

Your dentist says you have to have braces, and your parents agree. Before you lose it, here are some tips to make life better.

- Remember you're not alone. Braces are super-common, and lots of people have to wear them. Even if you're the first in your friend group to get braces, you won't be the last.
- Talk to your orthodontist. You might be able to get a type of braces that aren't super-ugly or uncomfortable. There are lots of options these days! Some are even "invisible."
- Sometimes braces can be uncomfortable when they are first placed or when they get adjusted. Try to prepare by stocking up on foods that you enjoy even when chewing isn't fun: ice cream, anyone?
- Follow the rules. Your doctor will show you how to brush, floss, and otherwise keep your smile bright even though your teeth are locked up in a cage. If you don't keep it clean, you might end up with stained teeth in the long run, which could make you even more embarrassed!
- All things pass. You might have trouble talking or pronouncing certain sounds when you first get braces. Don't worry, this won't last. In the meantime, you can impress your friends with your silly new voice.
- Don't be self-conscious. Smile, laugh, and live your life knowing that you're going to have an even more beautiful smile when this is all over!

# OCCUPATIONAL HAZARDS

## (SURVIVING SCHOOL AND WORK)

# Dealing With Bullies

It's no fun getting picked on, pushed around, or beat up. Here are some tips that can help if you find yourself in trouble with bullies.

### 1. Keep Your Cool.
Be calm but assertive. Tell the bully to stop in a loud, clear voice. Then walk away. If this reaction sounds hard, practice what to say at home or with a friend.

### 2. Try Not to React.
Getting upset, crying, or yelling may only encourage the bully to keep acting up. No reaction from you = no attention for the bully.

### 3. Laugh It Off.
Many kids have escaped bullying by turning the situation into a laughing matter. Try agreeing with the bully in a joking manner, saying something silly, or just laughing in their face. You'll catch the bully off guard, entertain your friends, and hopefully escape unscathed.

> ⚠ **SAFETY TIP: Anger Management**
> If you find yourself about to blow your top, do anything you can to create your own time-out. Walk away and find a quiet place to take some slow, deep breaths. Picture your self in a relaxing spot, where you always feel calm and happy. Try counting backward from one hundred. Depending on the situation, you might even play a quick game or do a puzzle to get your attention focused elsewhere.

### 4. Tell an Adult.

Adults need to know right away that bullying is happening. If you're being bullied at school or on the bus, tell a teacher, counselor, or even the principal. If the bullying is happening in your neighborhood, tell a parent or trusted adult. If the first person you tell doesn't do something to help, tell someone else.

### 5. Safety in Numbers.

Bullies often strike when kids are alone. Try to stay in a group. Hang out with your friends or stay near a teacher or other adult.

### 6. Let's NOT Get Physical.

While it might be tempting to take a swing at the bully, this is not a great solution. First, you're reacting, which is just what the bully wants. Second, it can escalate the situation into violence and one or more people could be seriously hurt. Third, you'll probably get in lots of trouble. Try to keep your cool and walk away.

# Stop Bullying, Save the World?

There's a lot you can do to stop bullying and make the world a better place. Here are some dos and don'ts:

- **DO** step in if you see a bully in action. Tell them to stop, and make it clear you support the person being bullied.
- **DO** be kind to someone who is bullied. Invite them to sit with you at lunch or on the bus, hang out with them at recess, or invite them to do something after school.
- **DO** let adults know if you see bullying.
- **DO** treat everyone with respect.
- **DO** talk to teachers or your school principal about starting an anti-bullying club or another way to stop bullying.
- **DO** put yourself in the bully's shoes. Many bullies are picked on themselves. Being kind to a bully might help them change their ways.
- **DO** apologize if you've bullied anyone or said mean things to them.
- **DON'T** stay quiet. Speaking up will let the bully know their behavior is not okay.
- **DON'T** be mean. Find something else to do instead of picking on someone.
- **DON'T** treat someone badly because they're "different." We all have our quirks.

Bullies in Cyberspace

Getting bullied online can take many forms, but all can make a person feel unsafe and scared. If you're being cyberbullied, take these steps:

- Tell an adult right away.
- Mute or block the person or people who are harassing you.
- Cyberbullies want a reaction from you. Don't give it to them. It's hard, but ignoring these meanies is the best bet.
- Collect evidence. Save mean texts or messages, and screenshot nasty posts or photos.
- Ask an adult to contact your internet or phone provider. These companies have tools to track down and stop cyberbullies.
- Take a break. Staying offline for a while might allow the situation to calm down.
- NEVER share your passwords with anyone. You never know who might want to use it against you.
- Be careful what you post online. Anything you say can and will be used against you.
- Privacy settings let you control who sees your posts online. Make your settings as private as possible to limit weirdos from stalking or harassing you.

# Mean Teachers

You're not sure why, but Mr. Meanie is out to get you. He's constantly yelling at you in class and giving you bad grades. Or Ms. Angrypants makes fun of you for giving a wrong answer and freezes you out of class discussions, then says you don't participate. What's a poor student to do?

**Check Yourself.** Are you doing things that make the teacher angry? Are you late for class, not paying attention, muttering under your breath? Ask around and see if anyone is noticing you doing something that might be drawing negative attention.

**Put Yourself in Their Shoes.** Think about what might make the teacher so angry all the time. Maybe he doesn't feel well or has trouble at home. Maybe she is tired of rude students or just burned out. Having compassion goes a long way.

**Show You Care.** Pay attention, speak up in class discussions, turn in your homework on time, and generally act like you're interested (even if you have to fake it sometimes!).

**Get the Scoop.** It's not you—some teachers are just grouchy. Talk to older siblings or other students who've had this teacher before and get some tips. They might have some strategies that will help you. Who knew Ms. Nasty loves to see pictures of students' pet cats and dogs, or Mr. Yellsalot loves knock-knock jokes? Tips like these can help make the classroom a friendlier place.

**Talk It Over.** Ask the teacher if you can talk privately before or after class. Be polite and respectful. Your teacher might appreciate the effort and give you points for being mature.

**Ask, Don't Argue.** Instead of saying, "I know you hate me," ask the teacher, "What steps can I take to do better in class?" or say, "I feel like I may have made you angry. What can I do to make things better?"

**Apologize if Necessary.** Tell the teacher you're sorry about that cartoon you drew of him as an ogre, or apologize for that hurtful joke you made. Promise to be more polite in the future—and then follow through!

**See the Big Picture.** Your teacher might have a reason for being tough on you. Maybe they think you're not doing your best work and they want to push you to do better. Putting more effort into your work and classroom behavior might solve the problem.

**Document, Then Escalate.** If none of these tips help and you really feel the teacher is singling you or others out for bad treatment, it's time to step up your game. Keep a record of mean comments and actions, noting dates and times when the teacher made fun of someone or acted unfairly. Then speak to the principal, dean, or another school big shot about what's happening. Having facts to back up your argument will help you get taken seriously. Of course, you should let your parents know what's going on as well.

**Safety in Numbers.** If you do go up the chain of command, ask your classmates to help you. Having a group express their concerns is likely to be taken more seriously than just one unhappy student.

**Make a Break for It.** If all else fails, ask (or have your parents ask) to be transferred to a different class. Sometimes getting a new perspective is the best way to solve a problem.

# Testing Troubles

You have a monster test coming up and you're overwhelmed with how to study. Are you going to fail and be stuck in school for the rest of your life? Not likely, espccially if you take these steps:

- Take notes and use them.
- Don't wait till the last minute. Break the material into small sections and study some of it each day leading up to the test.
- Find a strategy that works for you. For example, writing out class notes by hand often helps students learn better.
- Make studying fun. Reward yourself after you complete a chapter, or make up silly games, pictures, or rhymes to help you remember facts and dates.
- Find your space. Some people need complete quiet when they study, while others find listening to music helps them focus. Find what works for you and make it happen.
- Join a study group. Working with other students can help you understand things better.
- Make flash cards to quiz yourself on memorizing important vocabulary, dates, facts, or formulas.
- Ask for help. Let the teacher know you're having trouble— they may have resources or tips that can help.

- Get a tutor. Whether it's your big sister, the high school student next door, or a professional teacher, extra help from a tutor can make a big difference.
- Eat a good, healthy meal before your test. Good food will help you focus—and stop those distracting tummy rumbles!
- Get a good night's sleep before the test.
- Look over the test before you start. Do the easy questions first.
- Figure out how much time you have to write that essay or complete each section so you don't panic later on.
- If you have time once you've finished, read through the test again and check to make sure you didn't miss any questions. Double-check your answers—you may find you have something to add or left out a word.

# Cheater Cheater

What's the best way to get out of a cheating situation? It's simple—don't cheat to begin with! Cheating could mean bringing in the answers to a test, copying a classmate's work, copying and pasting text off the internet, even using artificial intelligence to write your paper. No matter what form it takes, cheating is dishonest and just plain wrong.

## Caught Red-Handed

- Understand that what you did was wrong.
- Admit guilt. Don't try to blame someone else or lie about or explain away what happened.
- Tell the teacher why you cheated. Did you not study? Are you worried about what your parents would say if you failed? Is school stress just getting too overwhelming?
- Take the consequences of your actions without throwing a tantrum or overreacting. This is a situation of your own making.

- Ask what you can do to make things better. Can you rewrite the paper? Take the test over? Do an extra credit project?
- Remember how miserable you feel about getting caught and make a plan to avoid cheating in the future

## Unfairly Accused?

What if you're accused of cheating but you didn't do it? Here are your options:

- Stay calm. State that you did not cheat.
- Ask to see the evidence against you.
- Talk to your parents. Tell them what happened and ask them to support you.
- Meet with the teacher and principal to present your side of the story.

# But Everyone Is Doing It!
# (Dealing With Peer Pressure)

Everyone wants to feel accepted and liked. Sometimes that means doing what your friends and classmates are doing. Unfortunately, following the crowd can get you into trouble. Want to go your own way? Here are some ideas.

**See the Good.** Are your teammates doing extra workouts to improve their skills? Do your friends push you to speak up more or make friends with the new kid? That's the kind of peer pressure that can make you a better person. Look for examples of good peer pressure and follow the crowd.

**Avoid the Bad.** If your friends encourage you to be mean to someone, lie, steal, cheat, or do something dangerous, it's time to say no. And it's probably time to find some new friends.

**Everyone Is NOT Doing It.** "But everyone's doing it" sounds like a convincing excuse, but it really isn't. If everyone were doing something, you would already be doing it too!

**Just Say No.** Remember that 'No" is a complete sentence. You don't owe anyone an explanation for why you do or don't want to do something. If you feel uncomfortable about joining the crowd, just say no.

**Make Excuses.** If just saying no doesn't get you off the hook, it's okay to give an excuse. "Sorry, vaping makes my asthma worse." "The coach will kick me off the team if I'm caught." "I've got a big test tomorrow, so there's no way I can stay out late tonight." "My family is going away for the weekend so I can't come to the party." These are all perfectly good ways to keep the pressure off.

**Expand Your Social Circle.** If you're starting to feel uneasy or guilty about the things your friend group likes to do, look around for kids who you have more in common with, and find ways to hang out with them instead. Join a new club, team, or youth group; volunteer; or invite a classmate to hang with you after school one-on-one.

**Plan Ahead.** Think of ways to get out of a bad situation. Going to a party? Prepare what you'll say or do if people are drinking alcohol. Asked to give a friend the answers to a test? Practice saying "no" ahead of time.

**Blame Your Parents.** Parents are usually happy to take the fall, especially when it's something they don't want you doing anyway. Tell friends your parents will punish you if you dye your hair purple without asking or sneak out of the house after curfew.

**Listen to Yourself.** If your inner voice is telling you something is a bad idea, it probably is. And if you do something you know is wrong, you're just going to feel miserable afterward. Why make yourself unhappy?

**Prepare for the Consequences.** Sometimes not following the crowd means you get shut out for awhile. Yeah, it sucks to be treated this way, but hold your head up and ignore any teasing.

**Set a Good Example.** Lots of times, kids give into pressure even when they don't want to. If you say no, you can set a good example and help others find the courage to resist peer pressure too. Pretty soon, your classmates might be following you instead of following the crowd!

**Talk It Out.** If peer pressure is getting overwhelming, find an adult to talk to about it. It might be a parent, a friend's parents, a counselor, or a teacher. It doesn't matter who it is, as long as they support you.

# Internet Scams and Scares, Part I

It's a scary world out there, and that goes double for the internet. Here are some ways to stay safe while online.

### Keep It Private.
People can do bad things if they have your login and password info. Don't give those deets out to anyone (except your parents, if they like to keep an eye on your social media).

### Go Incognito.
Do you think your favorite actor or singer gives their personal phone number or other contact info out to just anyone? No way! So act like a celeb and keep personal information private. That means no sharing where you live, where you go to school, where you hang out on weekends, or where your parents live and work.

### Watch What You Post.
That innocent photo of your softball team shows the name of your town or school on your uniform. The camera on your computer picks up details in your room that identify where you live. Don't leave your camera on, and don't post photos with a lot of identifying details.

### Watch Out for Imposters.

You're having a great time chatting with someone new in your DMs. They've even sent you photos of themselves and want you to send your photo too. Watch out! That cute teen might actually be a creep in disguise.

### Scam Alert!

Have you ever gotten a message that you can win a million dollars if you just click on a link? Stop and think before you click. Anything that sounds too good to be true probably is, especially if the message comes from someone you don't know or a website you've never heard of.

### Look Before You Shop.

Before you buy that cool gadget or cute shirt you saw in an ad or sponsored post, do some research. Is the site reputable? Check reviews before you send your hard-earned money or banking info to a company you've never heard of.

⚠ **SAFETY TIP: Crash!**

Despite your best efforts, a hacker has gotten into your computer or you've picked up a nasty virus. What do do? Try these tips:

- Always back up important files onto another device or drive so you can restore them if needed.
- Disconnect your computer from Wi-Fi and power sources right away.
- Change all your passwords. Never repeat passwords or use the same password for multiple sites.
- Use security software to scan for viruses, malware, spyware, or anything suspicious.
- Restore your computer to factory settings, then download your files (the ones you backed up, remember?).
- Ask your parents to freeze debit and credit cards and alert the bank.

# Internet Scams and Scares, Part 2

### Know Your Friends.
Did you get a friend request from someone you've never heard of? Check them out first. If they say they're friends with your someone you know, make sure that's true.

### Keep 'Em Guessing.
Your screen name can reveal too much about you, especially when predators or hackers are on the prowl. Stick to boring names that don't reveal too many personal details, like your gender, age, or where you live.

### Don't Go Alone.
Thinking of meeting an online friend in the real world? Proceed with caution! That fun teen you've been chatting with might turn out to be a scary monster in real life. ALWAYS tell your parents when you're thinking about meeting an online friend. Better yet, bring them with you and make sure they meet your new friend too. NEVER go alone to meet someone you don't know.

### Watch What You Post.
The internet is forever, and anything you post there can and will be used against you. Even deleting a post doesn't mean it's gone for good! So think before you post that mean tweet about your classmate, or that rude joke or photo you took. If you wouldn't want your sweet grandma to see it, don't post it.

### No Blind Clicking!
NEVER click on a link, photo, video, or title from someone or some company you don't know. Don't download new apps (even that awesome-sounding free game!) onto your device without doing some checking. That link could be a portal to identity theft or a nasty virus.

### Do Not Enter.
Never give anyone remote access to your computer. They might say they're fixing a tech issue, but it's more likely they're introducing a virus or stealing your personal information.

### Block, Block, Block.
If someone is threatening you online—harassing you, sending nasty messages, stalking, or just making you uncomfortable, block that person from all your social media.

### Speak Up and Keep Track.
If you are having trouble with someone online, or receiving threatening or inappropriate messages or photos, tell your parents right away. If your tormentor is a classmate, tell your school too. Take screenshots and document any messages or photos they send. You can report online harassment to the police and to cybertipline.org, a national center that helps track down bad guys (and gals) online.

# Gym Class Confidence

For some kids, gym is their favorite class. For others . . . not so much. If a teacher with a really loud whistle isn't your thing, these tips can help:

**Try your best.** You might not be the star of the team, but you can always score points for effort.

**Exercise your sense of humor.** Did you just wipe out on the basketball court or run to the wrong end zone? Making a joke can ease the tension.

**Look for options.** Some teachers allow students to do an individual fitness routine instead of taking part in an organized sport. Find an activity you prefer and see if you can get credit for it.

**Look on the bright side.** You get to run around, maybe even outside, instead of sitting at a desk in a stuffy room and listening to a teacher drone on for a little while. It's a win-win!

**Compete against yourself.** You might never beat Superfit Sally in a race to the finish, but you can improve your times. Set goals that work for you and feel proud about achieving them!

**Cut the stink.** Some schools require showers after gym class, and some don't. If you don't shower, you can splash some water on your face or use wipes to clean up and smell a bit fresher. And of course, dirty gym clothes should go in the laundry, not sit in the bottom of your locker or bag for weeks!

# Making the Team . . . Or Not

So you've decided to try out for a team. Here are some things to work on as you work out.

- Practice, practice, practice. The more you train, the better you'll perform. And athletes with a great work ethic can beat natural talent in the long run.
- Talk to kids who are already on the team. Find out what to expect at tryouts.
- Bring a buddy. Trying out with a friend can help you feel more comfortable.
- Be prepared. Bring any equipment you might need and dress for the sport.
- Get mental. You need to train your brain as well as your body. Feeling confident and determined can go a long way toward success.
- Don't be embarrassed. You don't have to be the best to make the team, and it's okay if you missed a shot or messed up a play. This isn't the Olympics.
- Show good sportsmanship. Help other kids, be supportive, and show the coach you can work hard and take direction. Coaches love that!
- Perform for yourself. Don't be intimidated or feel scared if you see other kids doing better.
- Prepare to lose, hope to win! Not everyone can make the team. It's okay to feel bad, but don't let the outcome get to you. You can always try again next season!

# Speak Up!

It might not make sense, but speaking in public can make our stomachs lurch, our hands sweat, and our bodies tremble. Since taking a vow of silence isn't really a thing, here are some Dos and Don'ts to get you through your time in the spotlight.

- **DO** prepare ahead of time. Research and take notes so you feel confident that you know what you're talking about.
- **DO** practice. Give your speech to your family, your friends, even your pet goldfish.
- **DO** start strong. Begin your speech with a joke or a fun fact to get your audience's attention.
- **DO** look for distractions. Focus on a spot in the back of the room if you feel nervous making eye contact. Or look for a friend and speak to that person.
- **DON'T** mumble. Speak clearly so everyone can hear you.
- **DON'T** rush. We know you want to finish quickly but talking too fast will only annoy your audience.
- **DON'T** keep your head down. It's tempting to stare at the paper you're reading from, but it's boring for the audience. Find some friendly faces and make eye contact.
- **DON'T** forget to breathe. Deep breaths before your speech can help you feel calm and focused.
- **DO** reward yourself! You did it! Treat yourself to a favorite snack or game afterward.

# Vote for Me!

Do you dream of running for president—class president, that is? Here's a handy guide to running a successful campaign for school office.

- Think about why you want to run. Are there things at your school that you'd like to change? While making classes optional or changing the cafeteria menu to create an ice cream course at every meal probably won't fly, there are probably some real ways to make school more fair and more fun.
- Promote yourself. Ask your classmates to vote for you and spread the word through campaign posters and speeches. This is no time to be shy!
- Consider handing out fun promos, such as T-shirts or buttons with your campaign slogan.
- Be respectful of other candidates. Run a clean campaign with no name-calling, rumor-spreading, or nasty tricks.
- Remember that being in office is hard work. Be sure you have time to take on the job and do it well.
- If you lose the election, be gracious. Congratulate your opponent and ask them if there is any way you can help them run the school.

# Ahh! Stage Fright!

You'd love to have a part in the school play, but the idea of auditioning makes you want to dig a hole and hide there forever! Fear not! You can overcome audition anxiety and stage fright with these tips:

- Prepare for your audition. Get a copy of the script if you can. If you will be expected to sing, learn a song from the show or bring a piece you're familiar with.
- Practice with friends. It will be more fun, and you'll have support when you go to the audition.
- Breathe. It really will help you calm down.
- Take a walk. Before it's your turn, pop outside for a quick walk to clear your head and focus.
- Act confident. Confidence always makes a good impression.
- Didn't get the part you wanted? Enjoy the part you did get (even if it's just Sheep #5 or Chorus Member #52), and gain experience for next time!

⚠ **SAFETY TIP: Staying Upright on Stage**

It's surprisingly common for performers to feel faint on stage—and fainting is not the way you want to steal the show! Make sure you never perform on an empty stomach and that you're well hydrated before you go onstage. And if you do start feeling faint, first try shifting your weight and bending your knees—sometimes you just need to revive the circulation in your lower half. If that doesn't help, sit down, put your head between your legs, and take some deep breaths.

## Break a Leg

Hooray! You've made the show, but now you're terrified to get onstage. Here's how to tame the stage fright monster.

- Forget the audience. Yes, people are staring at you, but pretend the room is empty and you're acting, singing, or dancing just for fun.
- Understand it's okay to be nervous. If you weren't a little nervous, it might mean you don't care. And we know you DO care—a lot!
- Look for support. Talk to your parents, teacher, and friends about how you feel.
- Don't be self-conscious. Many times, when things go wrong onstage, the audience doesn't even notice. If you mess up, carry on like nothing is wrong.
- Be your own hype man (or woman). Remind yourself that you've practiced, and you know what you're doing. You've got this!

# Going to a Wake or a Funeral

Whether it's a relative, a family friend, or someone you don't know well at all, going to a wake or a funeral can be scary and upsetting. Here are some ideas to get through it.

**1. Talk It Over.**
Talk to your parents or another trusted adult about how you feel. It's okay to admit you're frightened. Ask an adult what to expect and what people might say or do.

**2. Be Prepared.**
The body might be on view at the wake, and the person probably won't look like you remember them. Although this can be confusing or upsetting, it is normal. And while some people might touch the body, you certainly don't have to if you don't want to.

### 3. Be Respectful.

Dress nicely. Tell the family or people closest to the person who died that you're sorry for their loss. If you want to approach the coffin, you may kneel and say a prayer, or you may just think quietly to yourself. If you're uncomfortable, it's fine to just sit in the back of the room.

### 4. Follow the Crowd.

If you've never been to a funeral or if it is a religious ceremony you aren't familiar with, it's fine to sit quietly and watch what other people do. You don't have to recite prayers or sing songs if you don't want to.

### 5. Share Memories.

If you have special memories of the deceased, you might want to share them with the family through a letter or video. Or you can remember the person in a special way, such as volunteering for a cause they believed in, drawing a picture, or doing an activity they loved.

> ⚠ **SAFETY TIP: Getting Through Grief**
> When someone dies, grief looks different for everyone. There is no right or wrong way to do it. Be patient with yourself and with others who have lost a loved one. The hurt can last for a long time. But hopefully good memories of that person will last even longer.

# You're Hired!

Are you ready for your first job interview? Here's how to ace the big meeting!

- Do your homework. Find out what the hours will be and what you're expected to do. Finding out how much you'll be paid is important too!
- Ask around. Do you have friends who have worked there? Ask them what the job is like.
- Practice. Do a mock interview with a parent, sibling, or teacher.
- Look sharp. Job interviews are not the place to wear your smelly gym clothes or the T-shirt you spilled spaghetti sauce on. Nice pants and a shirt will make a much better impression.
- Be on time.
- Shake hands with the person interviewing you and make eye contact. Don't slouch, look at your phone, chomp on gum, or pick your teeth.
- Explain why you want the job (other than "Because I need money") and why you would be a good choice.
- Be prepared for unexpected questions and try to think fast and answer them honestly.
- After the interview, it's polite to send a thank-you text, call, or email.

> ⚠ **SAFETY TIP: First Day Jitters**
> Congratulations, you got the job! But now it's your first day and you're not sure what do expect. Don't worry! Your new boss and coworkers will show you around and teach you what to do. Don't be afraid to ask questions if anything is unclear. Show up a little early, wear appropriate clothing, and get ready to learn and earn!

# Babysitting 101

Which word describes babysitting: Fun, Scary, Traumatic, or Fantastic? The answer is All of the Above! Take these tips along with you when you show up to watch someone else's kids.

- Take a babysitting or first aid class before you start taking jobs.
- Take it seriously. Your job is to keep the kids safe.
- Talk to the parents beforehand. Find out what they expect of you, if anyone has allergies, what the house rules are, and what the kids' routine is.
- Be clear about how much you're being paid and what time the parents will be home.
- Remember it's not party time. You should not have friends over (unless the parents specifically say it's okay), eat all of the family's snacks, or binge-watch your favorite show (unless the kids are asleep).
- Be prepared. Bring an activity bag with games, toys, coloring books, or crafting materials to play with.
- Keep important phone numbers on hand in case of an emergency.
- Be gentle but firm. Kids might try to break the rules, but it's your job to keep them in line. At the same time, don't be an ogre who scares the kids into submission.
- Be open to suggestions. Ask the parents if they have any concerns about your job.

# SOCIAL
# SITUATIONS

# Idle Gossip

Psst! Did you hear the one about the kid who gossiped so much, his tongue fell out? That story may not be real, but gossip is real, and it can make you miserable. Here's some tips to deal with the trash talk.

### I. Don't Play Telephone.
Have you ever played Telephone, the game where you whisper something in a person's ear, that person whispers it to the next person, and so on? By the time the last person hears the news, it's totally different from what you said in the first place! Gossip is the same way: statements get twisted and turn into crazy lies. So don't believe everything you hear.

### 2. Break the Chain.
It can be tempting to share the exciting news that Little Miss Perfect was caught cheating on a test. But, like we said, fact has a way of turning into fiction once gossip takes over. So don't repeat things you hear second- or third-hand, no matter how tempting. And if someone starts to tell you something juicy, staring at them and saying "Why are you telling me this?" can stop mean talk in its tracks.

### 3. Put Yourself in Their Place.
Before you speak, think about the person you're gossiping about. Are your words going to hurt them? Would they hurt you if the roles were reversed?

## 4. Stand Up for Yourself.

If people are gossiping about you, find out who started the rumor and tell Big Mouth to shut their, well, big mouth. Deny the rumor, but don't throw a tantrum. Acting crazy will only make you look more guilty.

## 5. Wait It Out.

Gossip usually dies out, or people find someone new to talk about. Ignore the fake news and let it fade away.

⚠ **SAFETY TIP: Favorite Gossip-Ending Phrases**
1. "I don't like talking about someone who isn't here to defend themselves."
2. "What do you mean by saying that?"
3. "What's the point of talking about this?"
4. "I don't think that's any of my business."
5. "BORING. What we should really be talking about is . . ."

Follow any of those up with a change in subject—hopefully to something more positive—and gossip, begone!

# Hello, My Name Is . . .

You've just moved to a new town or started a new school. Are you dreading being "the New Kid"? Fear not! These tips will help.

### 1. Start Fresh.
No one at your new school knows you once threw up in class or that you used to have a not-so-secret, over-the-top love of stuffed frogs. You can present a whole new image—of the real you that you are now, not your past—at your new school.

### 2. Get the Scoop.
Does the kid down the street go to your school? Do your parents know someone who already goes there? Try to find out all you can about your new school and teachers before you walk into class. If you can, tour the school before your first day so you don't have to stress about getting lost or finding your locker.

### 3. Go Undercover.
Spend the first few days getting the lay of the land. Observe and learn things like what kinds of friend groups gather where, what type of music is popular, and which teachers students seem to dread seeing in the hallways.

## 4. Be Cheerful.

Presenting a positive attitude, even when it's just a brave smile, goes a long way toward getting people to like you. Instead of moping or giving people the silent treatment, act like you really want to be there. And there's no better ice breaker than asking someone for help—most people like to be helpful!

## 5. Push Yourself.

You might feel shy, but don't be afraid to ask to sit near a classmate at lunch. If they say no, ask someone else.

## 6. Express Yourself.

Wearing a shirt featuring your favorite pop star or sports team can be a great way to find kids with similar interests.

## 7. Join In.

Joining after-school clubs or teams can help you make new friends with common interests.

## 8. Take Your Time.

You probably won't meet your new besties on the first day. It's okay to take time to settle in.

# Friendship Dos and Don'ts

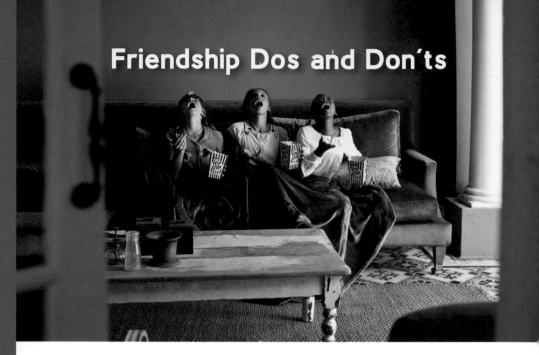

Friends. We all need them, but sometimes it's hard to find them. Want to improve your social life? Here's a few dos and don'ts.

- **DO** join in. Joining clubs, teams, or activist groups is a great way to meet people with the same interests as you.
- **DO** make conversation. Even a simple question like "Do you have any pets?" can start a friendship.
- **DO** compliment people. It's always nice to hear someone likes your hoodie or your hairstyle, and this can open up a new relationship.
- **DO** make plans. Get a group together to go to a game or the movies, or ask a few friends to form a study group.
- **DON'T** be a pest. Being clingy or overly demanding will be overwhelming to most people.
- **DON'T** fake it. Be true to yourself and your friends, and don't hang out with people you don't like just for the cool factor.
- **DON'T** get distracted. Constantly checking your phone or looking around the room is not just rude, it shows the other person you don't care about them.

- **DON'T** be a killjoy. No one wants a friend who complains, whines, or just isn't fun to be around. Try to have fun no matter what kind of day it is.
- **DON'T** limit yourself. If you're having trouble making friends in your classes at school, volunteer, take a class outside of school, or join a community group to meet your people.
- **DON'T** be a bad friend. Do you gossip or trash talk your friends behind their backs? Do you interrupt them or make every interaction about yourself? You have to be a good friend in order to have good friends!

# What to Do If You Lose a Friend

You had a bestie, but they moved away, or you find out they gave their extra ticket to the sold-out concert to someone else. Rejection hurts. Here's how to cope.

- **Own your feelings.** It's normal to feel sad, upset, or angry.
- **Find out what's going on.** Maybe your friend had a good reason for having a sleepover and not inviting you, or for giving you the cold shoulder at lunch. Catch them privately and ask if you've done something wrong.
- **Apologize if necessary.** You thought the joke you made about your friend's new prized possession was a riot, but they weren't amused. If you've hurt a friend's feelings, say you're sorry—and mean it.
- **Be cool.** It's okay to be upset. It's NOT okay to scream, yell, or get physical with your former BFF.
- **Look for support.** If you're feeling really blue, tell a parent, counselor, teacher, or other kids what's going on with you. They might have some ideas to help lift your mood.
- **Move on.** Look for new friends at school, or join clubs or groups where you can meet new people.
- **Remember, most friendships don't last forever.** It's normal to have different friend groups as you grow up. You'll find another bestie soon!

# The Popularity Contest

Let's face it: Some kids are popular and some kids aren't. There are some people who gather friends like honey gathers flies... okay, maybe that's not the best example! But it's true that kids who are attractive, athletic, or just super-confident usually seem to have the most friends. Is that fair? Maybe not, but as your parents probably love to say: "Life isn't fair!"

Do you want to be more popular? Don't be fake, but do look for ways to build your confidence. Maybe you're not great at sports, but you're a whiz at art or tech or theater. Or maybe you're kind, generous, and lots of fun to be around. These qualities can make you someone others want to hang with, especially if you find people who are interested in the same things.

Maybe you have the opposite problem: You feel like everyone hates you. Even if there's no way you can—or want to—be Captain Popularity, you can still find friends who like you and like spending time with you—and the feeling can be mutual! As we've said before, look for people who like the same things you do. If you don't find them at school, try community classes or clubs or volunteer work.

Remember, popular kids have stresses, worries, and problems, just like you do—just like everyone does! Being popular doesn't mean everything in life is automatically perfect.

# No Fighting!

You're arguing with a classmate and suddenly they start throwing punches or yelling insults. Take a deep breath and read these tips to take the situation back from one hundred to zero.

- Keep your cool. Instead of coming up with your own insults, just swallow that clever taunt and walk away.
- Sometimes you just want to slap someone silly, but that's almost always a bad idea. Resist the impulse to get violent or physical.
- Try humor. Sometimes a joke or a laugh can stop the flow of insults.
- Change the focus. If someone pushes you or says something mean, say something like, "I've got to go or I'll be late to class" or "Hey, did you see that game yesterday?"
- Tell a parents, teacher, or trusted adult if someone is harassing you physically or verbally. If the conflict has been going on for a while, ask a teacher or counselor to meet with both of you and come up with ideas to get along better.
- Don't get caught alone. Hopefully a fight won't escalate if you're hanging with your friend group or your family— you'll be hanging with them instead of the instigator.
- If someone gets violent with you, protect yourself by covering your head with your hands and arms. If you're knocked down, curl up into a ball to protect your belly.
- Check out the pages on dealing with bullies (pages 132–135) for more advice.

# Say You're Sorry!

Did you hurt someone's feelings with a snarky comment? Share a secret without permission? It's hard, but sometimes you have to swallow your pride and say those two tough words: "I'm sorry."

- Think about what you said or did and how it affected the other person. Look at the situation from the other person's point of view to see clearly why they're upset.
- Practice apologizing in private before you speak to the person you've hurt. Or role-play your apology with a parent or friend.
- Take responsibility for what you did. Instead of just mumbling "Sorry," try "I'm sorry I didn't invite you to the party. I understand that probably made you feel left out and sad."
- Apologize for your behavior, not for the other person's feelings. Saying "I'm sorry you're upset" doesn't address what you did.
- Avoid the word "but." "I'm sorry I called you that name, but you made me mad" isn't an apology; it's making an excuse and putting the blame on the other person.
- If it's hard for you to speak to the person, write a note or make a video for them instead.
- Try to make it up to the person. Offer to replace an object you've broken or invite them to a fun event.
- What if the person doesn't accept your apology? Repeat that you're sorry and let your actions show that you've learned from your mistake and changed your behavior.
- Move on. Don't beat yourself up, especially if the problem was caused by a mistake or happened accidentally.

# Dying of Embarrassment

We're pretty sure being embarrassed never killed anyone, but it's hard to remember that when you let out a noisy fart in front of someone you wanted to impress, or trip and spill your entire lunch on the floor in front of the whole cafeteria. Here are some ways to deal with the cringe.

### 1. Laugh It Off.
This is the best way to defuse the tension and show others you don't think what you did is a big deal. Or make a joke, like, "I guess I can never show my face in this town again!"

### 2. Stay Cool.
Crying, yelling, or running away are extreme reactions, and they'll just give the crowd something else to laugh about.

### 3. See the Big Picture.
Sure you're cringing because you wore a costume to your friend's party and everyone else was in sweats, but is it really the end of the world? Did your behavior injure anyone or cause a national emergency? Probably not, so move on.

### 4. Just Forget It.
You may never forget dropping your full lunch tray in the cafeteria, but odds are everyone else will get over it soon enough.

# Stressed Out

So you've got a big test on Thursday, you have tons of extra chores this week, and you think your best friend is mad at you. Sounds like a recipe for stress!

## Keep Calm and Carry On

- Think about what's stressing you out. Make a list of what's bothering you.
- Set priorities. If you feel over-scheduled, grab a calendar, and write down specific time periods for each activity or task you need to accomplish.
- Take a break. A long walk or a quick game can distract you and help you feel better.
- Breathe. Find a quiet place, clear your mind, and take deep breaths. Let your body relax. Think of a happy time or a place that makes you feel good.
- Reframe the situation. Instead of thinking, "I'll never understand these math problems!" try "I don't understand them yet, but I can find someone to help me until I get it."
- Talk it out. Maybe a sibling can help you with your chores, or you can ask a friend to help you study for that big test.
- Confide in a parent, counselor, or other trusted adult. They're sure to understand that stressed-out feeling and can help you deal with the struggle.
- Don't let stress affect your behavior. It's normal to feel like blowing your top or to act all moody around your friends, but that may only cause more problems—and more stress!

# Breaking Up Is Hard to Do

Life was great for a while, but suddenly your significant other isn't so interested in you, or you're not so happy being with them. Breaking up can be rough, but you can get through it!

### 1. Talk It Over.
Meet privately with your other half and calmly express what's bothering you. Try to reach an agreement about what to do going forward. Do you want to stay together? Make changes in behavior? Or is it time to go your separate ways? Only you can decide.

### 2. Stay Calm.
You may feel so angry or frustrated you could explode, but take a deep breath and don't scream or throw things.

### 3. Don't Blame or Shame.
It's easy to feel down on yourself after a breakup, but this is just one event in your life. Think of all the awesome things about yourself!

### 4. Distract Yourself.
Take up a new hobby, get into a new show or game, or join a club or volunteer organization. You'll be so busy you won't have time to think of You-Know-Who.

### 5. Lean on Others.
Your friends or family can help you feel better after a breakup, so spend some quality time with your gang.

### 6. Don't Be Cruel.
Spreading rumors or saying nasty things about your ex will only make you look bad or make a nasty situation worse. Remember, "If you can't say something nice, don't say anything at all."

### 7. See the Big Picture.
Most people have a number of relationships before they find their One True Love. Breaking up hurts, but there are other fish in the sea. You'll find someone special again.

### 8. Wait It Out.
With time, it will be easier to remember the fun times and everything you liked about each other in the first place. You may even get to be friends. But don't rush yourself or your ex to "just get over it." These things take time.

Ready to throw the party of the year? Here are some Dos and Don'ts to make your event the talk of the town—for all the right reasons.

- **DO** involve your parents from the start. Work together to figure out a budget, snacks, guest list, activities, and, most important—ground rules.
- **DON'T** have a party if no grownups are around. Unsupervised parties can turn into a nightmare.
- **DO** ask your parents to keep younger siblings busy and out of your hair unless you want them at the party.
- **DON'T** be a jerk if your parents want to check in to make sure the party stays safe and fun.
- **DO** use good judgment about the guest list. You don't want uninvited guests to crash the party, and you don't want anyone to feel like they missed out.
- **DON'T** wait till the last minute. Send invitations a few weeks before your party so your guests can mark their calendars. It'll give you—and all of your guests—something to look forward to.
- **DO** remind your guests about the party and find out who's planning to come.
- **DO** plan the menu. Is this a casual bash with snacks and sodas, a formal sit-down dinner, or a taco bar free-for-all? Your guests will want to know.

- **DON'T** sit in silence. Create an awesome playlist or ten that you can swap in and out depending on the mood. Make sure to include at least one with upbeat music to get the party started!
- **DO** be considerate of your neighbors and anyone else who lives with you. Keep the noise down, stay off other people's property, and clean up any messes your guests make.
- **DON'T** be shy. Mingle and talk to all your guests, not just your BFF.
- **DO** introduce guests to each other if they haven't met before. Try to go beyond names and give at least one detail so they have something to talk about. Do they both love a certain movie or have a hysterical younger sibling? News you can use!
- **DON'T** leave the mess for your parents to clean up.

# Sweet Dreams

While sleepovers can be fun—who can resist staying up all night watching movies and eating junk food with friends?—they can also be stressful and scary sometimes. Keep these tips in mind.

### 1. Make a Plan.
If you're invited to a sleepover, find out if anyone else will be there and what activities are planned. If you don't like the sound of things, it's okay to make an excuse and say no.

### 2. Move Out of Your Comfort Zone.
On the other hand, trying new things can be fun! Have an open mind and be willing to embrace the unexpected.

### 3. Get Parents Involved.
Let your parents know who will be at the friend's house. Don't throw a fit if they want to talk to the friend's parents or meet them beforehand. If you're the one throwing the party, follow any rules your parents set down.

### 4. Expect the Unexpected.
Your friend might have different sleeping arrangements than you're used to, or their parents might serve unfamiliar foods at dinner. Roll with the new experiences, be polite, and make the best of things.

### 5. Bring a Comfort Object.

Can't sleep without Sammy the Stuffed Sloth? Bring him along! Afraid you won't be able to fall asleep? Pack a favorite book and a flashlight or bring your mobile device and earbuds so you can pass time without disturbing others. (Don't forget your charger!)

### 6. Have an Escape Plan.

If you've tried your best but just can't stick it out all night, it's okay to call your parents to come pick you up. If you want to set up a code word or symbol with your parents ahead of time, just make sure you're on the same page so there aren't any mixed signals.

### 7. Be Cool.

Whether you're the one who leaves early, or your friend leaves your sleepover for some reason, don't feel embarrassed or make the other kids feel bad. You can always try again another time.

# Boo!

All your friends are going to see the new horror flick and you want to go too, but you really dislike being so scared that you want to crawl out of your own skin. There's no need to fear if you take these steps.

- Read reviews. Even if you don't want to reveal any spoilers, they can help you to know the basic plot and how scary things might get.
- Or let the movie be spoiled for you by reading the full plot summary online. (Just don't spoil it for everyone else!)
- Remember that it's a make-believe story. Whatever you see on the screen can't hurt you.
- Avoid your own triggers. Are you terrified of clowns? Then it's probably best to skip *Zombie Clowns From Outer Space*, even if your friends are dying to see it.
- Choose a seat near the end of the row or an exit in case you need to take a break. "I have to go to the bathroom" is always a good excuse.
- Prepare for scares. It wouldn't be much of a scary movie if you didn't get a little bit scared! Be ready for the shock and then laugh it off with your friends.
- It's okay to peek through your fingers or hide your face in a pillow when things get too intense.
- Distract yourself. Load up some yummy snacks or bring a fidget toy to get the nervous energy out.

# New Situations

Invited to a wedding? Going to a formal dinner? Facing unfamiliar food on your plate? Plan ahead to make the situation fun!

**Ask Ahead.** If you're going to a new type of social event for the first time, ask your parents or friends what to expect. Is there a dress code? What activities should you expect? How long will you be there? Know before you go, so you can relax and have fun.

**Look for Clues.** Watching other people is a great way to figure out what's going on. Can't figure out how to eat something at dinner? See if other people are eating with their fingers or using a knife and fork.

**Don't Be Embarrassed.** So you used the wrong utensils at dinner, or forgot to stand up at the right moment during a ceremony. Honestly, you probably aren't the center of attention, so most people won't even notice.

**Hang With the Crowd.** Being with your family or friends can make you feel less awkward. There really is safety in numbers!

**Take a Break.** Feeling overwhelmed or bored? Devise a signal with your parents or friends that tells them, "I need to go outside for a few minutes."

**Be Adventurous.** Trying new things can lead to fantastic experiences! You might discover your new favorite food or find out you love dancing at the wedding reception. And you'll get to add another first to your growing list of lifetime experiences!

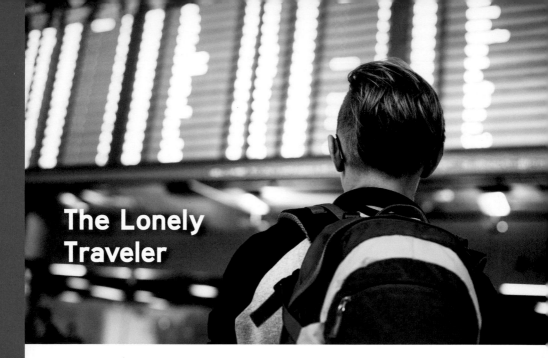

# The Lonely Traveler

Ready to take your first solo trip? Whether it's flying across the country to see a relative, or taking the bus to a friend's house, here are some tips to make traveling alone a good trip.

### I. Stay in Touch.
Have a list of contacts in your phone or in your backpack and make some plans for when they should each expect to hear from you. You'll feel better if you have a friend or family member waiting for your call. And they'll feel better when they know that you arrived safely.

### 2. Pack Light.
It will be easier and less stressful if you don't have to keep track of twenty bags or drag a two-ton suitcase through a crowded airport.

### 3. Bring Distractions.
Mobile devices, books, and games are a good way to pass the time and keep from getting bored or anxious. Don't forget your headphones or earbuds! The entire plane does NOT want to watch your movie with you.

### 4. Bring Snacks.
A bag of chips or favorite sweets makes everything better. And don't forget your water bottle!

### 5. Know the Plan.
Going over where to go, what to do, and what to expect before you leave home will make you feel more confident once you're on the road.

### 6. Be Aware.
Does the train station seem sketchy? Hang out near the ticket counter. Is the person sitting next to you on the plane making you nervous? Head to the restroom or become best friends with the flight attendant. Don't hesitate to ask for help.

### 7. Expect the Unexpected.
Your flight may be delayed, or you might miss a connection. Discuss potential problems with your parents so you'll know what to do. It's a good idea to make an adult, such as a ticket agent, flight attendant, or conductor, aware of your problem and ask for help.

### 8. Plan for Next Time.
Were there problems or mix-ups on your trip? Talk about them with your parents and brainstorm some ideas you can use to make your next trip better.